PASTORAL NOMADISM IN ARID ZONES OF INDIA

Pastoral Nomadism in Arid Zones of India

Socio - Demographic & Ecological Aspects

R.R. Prasad

1994

Discovery Publishing House

New Delhi - 110 002

First Edition 1994

ISBN 81-7141-237-8

Published by :
Discovery Publishing House,
4594/9, Darya Ganj, New Delhi - 110002

Laser Typesetting by :
Computer Codes,
Virat Bhawan, Comml. Complex, Mukerjee Nagar, Delhi-9

Printed at :
Efficient Offset Printers,
Delhi

CONTENTS

PREFACE

Arid areas essentially are lands of high risk and uncertainty. Pastoral nomadism in arid areas occurs as an ecological response to an unfavourable habitat. Nomadic way of life in its combination with nomadic livestock management is a very ancient form of adaptation to arid and semi-arid environments. The traditional system of economic production in arid areas, such as agriculture and pastoralism, had been well integrated and synergestic. The settled and nomadic pastoralist populations in past provided checks against excessive resource exploitation mainly through less intensive landuse, and, hence, maintained an ecological equilibrium. However, with the passage of time the ecological equilibrium is breaking down due to increased population growth of both humans and livestock and irrational landuse. This has made nomadic pastoralism an extremely difficult avocation to be maintained in the arid environment. This treatise has attempted to understand the implications of socio-demographic and ecological factors on the pastoral nomads in the arid zones of north-western India.

In carrying out this study I have received assistance from a number of individuals and organisations. While it is difficult to acknowledge all of them individually, I would like to record my profound gratefulness to the following persons.

At the outset, I acknowledge my deep sense of gratitude to Dr.Camilla Toulmin of the International Institute for Environment and Development, London for financing the research study and publication of this book. I am also thankful to Dr. Jeremy Swift of the Institute of Development Studies, Sussex for giving initial impetus for taking up this study.

Thanks are also due to Shri T.L. Sankar, Former Director General, NIRD and Shri A.V.S. Reddy, Dy.Director General, NIRD for providing encouragement and all the necessary support in carrying out this study. I am also indebted to Dr.K.C. Alexander and Dr. B.C. Muthayya, Director (Sociology) Director (CBOD), respectively, of NIRD for their valuable guidance.

My special thanks are due to Shri D.S. Rathore who worked as a consultant in this project. I received substantial help from Prof. Anil Gupta, I.I.M., Ahmedabad, Dr.L.P. Bharara, CAZRI, Jodhpur, Dr.D.B.Kalra, CSWRI, Avikanagar, Dr. Panjab Singh, Director, IGFRI, Jhansi, and Dr.Nahar Singh, Dy.Director, Sheep & Wool Department, Government of Rajasthan, Jaipur. I record my deep sense of gratitude to all of them.

I am immensely thankful to my colleague Shri G. Rajanikanth who helped me at the initial stage in collecting secondary data for the project.

I also wish to thank Shri D. Jayanandam, Cartographer, NIRD for preparing maps, and to Shri Ch.V.R.R. Vara Prasad and Shri B. Srinivasulu for typing the report.

AUTHOR

LIST OF TABLES

LIST OF FIGURES

1

Introduction

Introduction

Nomadism is as old as the history of mankind. Apart from the compulsions of nature and search for food, quest for knowledge and explorations of the unknown regions have led people to move from place to place and interact with different groups of people. There is a wide variety of nomadism across the world. India presents an unique array of nomadism connected with its ancient civilisation.[1]

Most of the dictionaries gave the meaning of the word nomad as a wandering pastoral community. But the term has a wider connotation as several supportive terms are being used along with it to distinguish one set of nomads from the others. The first edition of Encyclopaedia of Social Sciences (Vols.11-12) classifies nomads in three categories, namely, **hunting and collecting nomads, pastoral nomads, agricultural nomads** (1933:390). In the revised edition of the International Encyclopaedia of the Social Sciences (1968) nomadism has been dealt under two headings, namely, **hunting and gathering,** and **pastoralism** (Vols.7-8 and 11-12). It is argued that while to a certain extent nomadism is imposed on the former, the latter's movements are relatively culturally determined. Encyclopaedia Britanica (1961, Vol.16) states that modern term nomad is applied to all wandering peoples of which there are three main types, namely, **primitive nomads, pastoral nomads, tinker or trader nomads. Bacon**[2] takes the periodicity of movements into consideration and classifies them as true nomad; semi-nomad and semi-sedentary. **Misra**[3] made two broad divisions, namely, **symbiotic nomads** and **natural nomads** .

In understanding nomadism, the reason why people should habitually move is of primary importance. The other factors like where they move, how they move, what is the duration of their movement and what they do when they move are secondary and related to this factor. The ecological conditions, the culture of the neighbouring settled population and the nature of the relationship between the nomads and the neighbouring settled population are also of great significance in determining the various social, economic, political and religious features of a nomadic population.

In India both nomads and settled populations have been on the scene for many millennia. According to Sankhalia[4] and Thapar[5] the prehistoric record indicates that the Indian sub-continent supported hunters-gatherers until circa. 3000 B.C. Using the archaeological and ethnohistorical evidence, **Murthy and Sontheimer**[6] have examined the basis of nomadism in the Deccan Plateau: "... there is enough archaeological evidence to know the pre- history of early human populations that inhabibated this region. In Pleistocene and early Holocene times, they were conditioned to nomadic food procuring systems based on hunting and food gathering. By around the third millennium B.C., a food producing system based on a pastoral-cum- agricultural economy was introduced into this hunting and food gathering ecosystem by communities who moved in from elsewhere and raised villages in the favourable ecological niches. Some of the excavated settlements ... have shown that their economy was chiefly based on cattle pastoralism supplemented by agriculture and hunting." Once settled villages came onto the scene as a regular way of inhabitation the basis for interactions among the people living in different communities was established through exchanges of goods and services which could not be obtained in a single settlement.

Archaeological evidence from the **Indus Valley**[7] and Lothal[8] clearly indicate the development of transport and commerce in ancient India. **Wheeler**[9] notes: "... the gold used for beads, fillets and other ornaments by the **Harrappans** may thus have come at least in part through trade channels, some of it probably from South India. Who were these traders? What was the mechanism of their activities? How did they move and with what frequency? We have very little or no information on these questions. But it appears that in ancient India, apart from pastoral nomads, there developed a class of spatially mobile specialists who provided various kinds of goods, services and entertainments among more settled populations. They have been referred to in early **Vedic** literature, the **Rig Veda** referring to a number of specialized trades, crafts, entertainers etc., during the period circa 1000 - 700 B.C. Tamil Sangam literature spanning a period between circa 1 A.D. - 600 A.D., refers to a number of itinerants visiting villages and towns.[10] Recent Surveys in India, Pakistan and elsewhere show a large number of spatially mobile groups who adopt a variety of strategies for their subsistence.

One of the issues generated by the growing research record is that pastoral and non-pastoral nomads are qualitatively different and should be clearly distinguished. In the past, **non-pastoral** nomads have been variously labelled and often lumped under terms such as **wanderers** and **itinerants.** As knowledge about them is improved it has been realized that their movements are not sporadic or haphazard and they are neither aberrations or marginals.

The activities of nomads, pastoral or non- pastoral, are in continuous interaction with the environment and the surrounding settled populations giving rise to new situations which in turn motivate them to devise new strategies for survival. In turn, these new strategies and resources alter patterns of social organization and group structure.[11]

Transhumance

Nomadism, though very widespread and apparently haphazard, is in reality a very specialised system, and the apparently most specialised form of nomadism is **transhumance.** Transhumance is the regular seasonal movement of flocks between summer and winter pastures. The main distinction between transhumance and true nomadism is not that transhumance follows a fixed route, but that it involves a fixed abode for part of the year. It was defined by **Carrier**[12] as ‘a periodic and alternating displacement of flocks between two regions of differing climate’, though in fact the displacement is usually one of altitude, and is made to avoid great variations in climate. The term was coined by French geographers from **trans** (across) and **humus** (ground) and was originally applied to the twice-yearly flock movements of the Spanish Mesta. In 'normal' transhumance the winter home in the lowlands is the permanent one, while in 'inverse' transhumance the permanent home is the summer location in the mountains.

Jacobeit[13] stressed that the basic cause of transhumance was natural, and that social, economic and ethnographic factors were secondary.Transhumance created an independent spirit among shepherds and served as a means of preserving ancient traditions.

Pastoral Nomadism

Pastoralists are people who derive most of their income or sustenance from keeping domestic livestock in conditions where most of the feed that their livestock eat is natural forage rather than cultivated fodders and pastures. In most cases, pastoralists devote the bulk of their own, and their families working time and energy to looking after their livestock rather than to other economic activities. Pastoral **areas** are areas used by pastoralists and **pastoralism** is the term used to describe their way of life and their economic and land-use systems.[14] Mobility is an essential feature of pastoralism.

Many scholars distinguish between pastoralists who live entirely on the products of their livestock, and agriculturists who grow only plant crops. In fact, many pastoral groups grow some crops, and most agriculturalists have a few domestic animals. **Carrier**[15] pointed out that an entirely pastoral diet is rare, and pastoralists trade their products for grain.

Why some pastoralists practise nomadism? Pastoral nomadism occurs as an ecological response to an unfavourable habitat. It is practised where seasonal variations in temparature, in rainfall, in the incidence of diseases, in the growing, reopening and harvesting of crops, makes livestock-keeping in one area relatively more or less attractive than in another area according to a regular and predictable seasonal timetable. Livestock that move from one area to another according to the incidence of the rains can profit by feeding on the grazing when it is in its best condition as to palatability and protein content. Livestock may cause serious damage to crops in the cultivation zone around the pastoral areas during the growing and harvesting seasons; nevertheless they are welcome there after harvest because of their role in converting crop residues and other vegetation to manure and they can also obtain quite a high proportion of their annual feed intake there once the crops have been harvested. Nomadic movements are also made so as to produce high temporary densities of people and livestock where this is required for self-defence or because there are economies of scale. Perhaps most important of all, nomadic movements are made from one area to another because the one area has received, in this year or this season, relatively less rainfall than it normally does compared to the other.[16]

Pastoral Nomadism in Arid Zones of India

Livestock raising is the predominant occupation of the population inhabiting dry areas of the world. Associated with it, pastoral nomadism is important to greater or lesser extent in most of the arid and semi-arid regions of the Indian sub-continent. In the Great Thar Desert of northwest India, and throughout Rajasthan State as a whole, there are breeders and herders of livestock who depend largely upon natural pasture for nourising their animals. In Rajasthan, as in most of India, such pastoralists are integrated into a wider complex society, and are part of an elaborate division of labour.

The pastoralists of Rajasthan are based in villages, and share the villages and village lands with agriculturists and with craft and service specialists. Unlike the tribally organized pastoralists of Africa and the Middle East, those in Rajasthan have no territory of their own, no region over which they have primary claim or control. Unlike the market oriented ranchers of the North American West and Latin America, the pastoralists of Rajasthan do not own large areas of pasture land upon which their livestock can graze uncontested. The social, occupational, and productive environments of specialist pastoralist is thus a mixed one, with multiple distinctions and sometimes conflicting claims upon local resources; agricultural production, craft activities, pastoral exploitation, and general household maintenance co-exist in close proximity.

The pastoralists of Rajasthan make up something less than 5% of the village population, are in large portion, members of traditional herding castes, and own about 50% of the livestock. Livestock are grazed on village pasture and harvested fields, and on fallow land and waste land, and they are grazed on pasture and fields, fallow and waste, away from their home area. Few pastoralists own much land, and of that which is owned, as much as possible is cultivated with subsistence crops, especially cereals, such as millets, and pulses. Pastoralists from the Jodhpur district own small patches of land for cultivation, and depend upon permission from members of agricultural castes for access to grazing land, although a few individuals are beginning to purchase pasture land. In the Luni Basin, livestock specialist hold on average 3 Hectares of land, about half of that held by agriculturists.

Livestock migration is a predominant characteristic of arid and semi-arid areas of Rajasthan. It is considered to be an ameliorative measure of drought and practised by the livestock raisers for generations. Various groups like **Raikas, Jats, Seervi, Bishnoi, Rajputs, Gujjars and Sindhi Muslim** are the most predominant pastoral nomads of the area. These communities have ecologically adjusted at a particular technological level to utilise the marginal resources which occur in areas too dry, too elevated, or too steep for agriculture to be viable mode of livelihood.

Recent Trends in Pastoralism

The pattern of semi-nomadic pastoralism has been undergoing a change during the last few decades. Change is taking place in the occupation of the formerly nomadic livestock breeders and a gradual reduction in the size of their flock. The rapidly growing population has inflated the demand for wood for different purposes, whereas it has reduced the area under fallows, wastelands and forests. All these factors indicate the trend towards an increasing scarcity of resources in the arid areas. There are several reasons which may be attributed to this trend. Further, with the extension of area under cultivation, the extent of area available for grazing has gone down tremendously. This has disturbed the balance and the breeders find it difficult to raise large herds.

Information Gap

Existing recent literature on pastoral nomadism fails to offer adequate insight into the ecological compulsions which are adversely affecting the socio-economic condition of the pastoral nomads, their regular migrations, etc. Similarly, there is knowledge gap in the area of the effects of the seasonal migrations on the grazing lands and forests and management aspects of these through migratory routes. Again, there is very limited information available on the pasture area such as its extent, types, fodder potential, incidence of grazing and the problems connected with pasture management. On the other hand, no detailed study has been made of the nomadic graziers themselves, the nature and extent of livestock migration, effects of livestock migration on forests, social parameters of livestock migration, social organization, the migratory routes they follow, their land tenure system, difficulties they encounter and the human, social and ecological problems associated with pastoral nomadism. There was, therefore, a need to examine all these aspects in greater detail. The present study is an attempt in this direction.

Objectives

The objectives of the study are to:

(a) examine the various aspects of the ecological and economic adaptation of the pastoral nomads.

(b) discover the fundamental process whereby the pastoral nomads' forms of organizations are evolved and maintained.

(c) understand whether the stability of the pastoral nomads is being threatened due to the disturbances in the balance between pastures, animal population, and human population.

(d) assess whether there is a trend pointing in the direction of sedentarisation and the gradual giving up of nomadic life by pastoralists on account of experiencing a phase of severe involution reflected in the declining resources and productivity.

(e) study the stimulus provided by the pastoral crisis for innovation and development of new institutions keeping in view the needs and aspirations of the pastoral groups, their skills, customary modes of action and the social framework within which they function.

Methodology

Both primary and secondary data for the study have been collected. Primary data have been collected with the help of interview, participant and non-participant observation methods among various pastoral nomadic communities of Rajasthan and Gujarat. A few case studies have also been conducted. Since the subject of pastoral nomadism cuts across many disciplines like forestry, land- use, agriculture, grass, fodder and rangeland management, livestock management and environment, etc. a substantial amount of secondary data—both published and unpublished, have also been collected to explain the socio-demographic and ecological aspects of pastoral nomadism.

The study was conducted mainly in the districts of Jodhpur, Jaissalmer, Barmer of Rajasthan State and Kuchch district of Gujarat State. With a view to interviewing the pastoral nomads in different locations during their migration, visits to the district of Jaipur and Bharatpur in Rajasthan, Jhansi and Jalun in Uttar Pradesh State, and Raisen and Bhopal districts of Madhya Pradesh State were made. Besides, discussions with various livestock specialists, forest officers, arid zone research scientists, fodder and grassland management experts, etc. were also done to understand the implications of pastoral nomadism on ecology and demographic aspects.

Summary of Chapters

The present study report has been organised into seven chapters. The first chapter is the Introduction which deals with the origin and nature of nomadism and pastoral nomadism in a wider context. The second chapter deals with the pastoral nomadism in the arid zones of western India. In the third chapter, the implication of demographic factors on pastoral nomadism have been dealt with. Similarly, the impact of demographic factors on landuse, grass, fodder and rangelands availability and their implications on pastoral nomadism have been dealt with in the fourth chapter. The patterns of pastoral nomadism and its changing trends have been examined in fifth chapter. The sixth chapter deals with the impact of pastoral nomadism on the ecology of arid, semi-arid and humid areas, and the resultant problems for the pastoral nomads and steps suggested and taken to solve them. Finally the summary and conclusions of the study have been given in the seventh chapter. At the end of the each chapter, references cited have been given.

REFERENCES

1. Misra, P.K. 1982. Nomads in India, **Anthroplogical Survey of India,** Calcutta.

2. Bacon, R.H. 1954. Types of Nomadism in Central and South-east Asia, **South-western Journal of Anthropology,** Vol. 10.

3. Misra, P.K. 1969. Nomadism in India. **Journal of Indian Anthropological Society,** No.4 : 79 - 80.

4. Sankhalia, H.D. 1974. Prehistory and Protohistory of India and Pakistan. **Deccan College**. Poona.

5. Thapar, B.K. 1978. Early Farming Communities in India. **Journal of Human Evolution** 7:11-22.

6. Murthy, M.L.R and G. Sontheimer 1980 Prehistoric Background to Pastoralism in the Southern Deccan in the Light of the Oral Traditions and Cults of Some Pastoral Communities. **Anthropos** 75.

7. Wheelar, Mortimer. 1953. The Cambridge History of India. The Indus Civilization. Cambridge. **Cambridge University Press.**

8. Rao, S.R. 1973. Lothal and Indus Civilization. Bombay. **Asia Publishing House.**

9. Op. cit, Wheelar, M. 1953

10. Misra, P.K. and R.Misra. 1982. Nomadism in the Land of Tamils Between 1 A.D and 600 A.D. In Nomads in India. P.K. Misra and K.C. Malhotra, editors. Calcutta. **Anthropological Survey of India.**

11. Op.cit Misra, P.K. 1982. Nomads in India.

12. Carrier, E.H. 1932. Water and Grass : A study of the Pastoral Economy of Southern Europe. **Christophers,** London.

13. Jackobeit, W. 1961. Schafhatung and Schafer in Zentraleuropa bis zum Beginn des zo. **Johrhunderts.** Akademic-Verlag E. Berlin.

14. Standford, Stephen. 1983. Management of Pastoral Development in the Third World. **John Willey & Sons.** New York.

15. Op. cit Carrier, E.H. 1932

16. Op. cit Standford, Stephen. 1983.

2

Pastoral Nomadism in Arid Areas

Arid areas essentially are lands of high risk and of uncertainty. Under their generally clear, bright skies the scarcity and variability of rainfall are dominant elements in the complex of physical factors that set the stage upon which man ventures his livelihood, but the precise kind of risk is completely diversified, the range of uncertainty is great, and each sector of the zone provides its own special problems and opportunities for human occupation.[1]

Characteristically, the equalibrium of water, soil, geological and vegetative processes in arid lands is a delicate one, so that a slight shift in one aspect — such as grazing of vegetation — may set in motion a disastrous chain of events. Several themes thus run through the drama of man's occupation of arid lands. One is the unity of the area in terms of the general risks of rainfall deficiency and variability. A second is the diversity of the area in specific combinations of physical and cultural environment in which man deals with those risks. A third is the area's high sensitivity to radical readjustments triggered by a small change in the complex. The chief hazards which man faces in arid areas and which he tries to counter with many strategies are the risk of variation in precipitation and the uncertainty of its time of occurrence.

While it is customary to think of the arid lands as being sparsely populated, the density in fact ranges from zero in some of the great uninhabited portions of the continents to several of the most densely settled concentrations. Indeed, sharp discontinuities are the rule. Closely related to population densities but not directly coincident with them is the pattern of predominent livelihoods.

Most widespread is the nomadic herding of the Sahara, Arabia and South-west and central Asia. In effect, this has two sub-types, the complete nomad such as the Ouled Biri of Mauritania who with no permanent base follows the rains, and, much more common and dry fodder-producing areas or who are based on centres. This is wholly missing in the Americas and is one of the drastic distinctions between arid lands of the New and Old worlds. Either form of nomadism requires the pastoralists to order his livelihood so that he can survive the extreme draughts if he is to retain his crops, and in some places he may do some dry farming when the rains permit.

There has been no generally satisfactory subdivision of the arid lands according to the environmental complexes. The diverse patterns of population and livelihood in the arid areas correspond to climatic patterns in some areas but not in others, and it is important to recognise the profound differences in combinations of climate, landform, soil, vegetation and hydrology that are found within the limits of the arid lands.[2]

Arid Areas of India

THE arid region of India covering about 3.1 square lakh km is roughly 12% of country's total geographical area, and is spread over 7 states, namely **Rajasthan, Gujarat, Haryana, Maharashtra, Karnataka, Andhra Pradesh** and portions of **Jammu and Kashmir** (Fig. 1). The Indian and region lies between 24° and 29° N latitudes and 70° and 76° E longitudes. However, most (90%) of the Indian arid zone is located in north- western India (Fig. 2). About 62% of extremely arid region is predominantly located in 11 districts **(Barmer, Bikaner, Churu, Jaisalmer, Jodhpur, Jalore, Jhunjhunu, Ganganagar, Nagaur, Pali and Sikar)** of western Rajasthan (Table 1).

Archaeological evidences suggest that the onset of aridity was the major cause of the extinction of the **Riparian** and **Harappa-Kalibangan** civilization. A well-knit river system existed in the desert until recent times. The deterioration of climate, the rise of the **Himalayas**, the lowering of the **Aravallis**, important changes in the river systems, e.g. the diversion and disappearance of three classical rivers (the **Yamuna,** the **Saraswati** and the **Ghaggar**), and the lowering of the underground water-table caused increased aridity in the area.[3] **Krishnan**[4] observed that arid conditions might

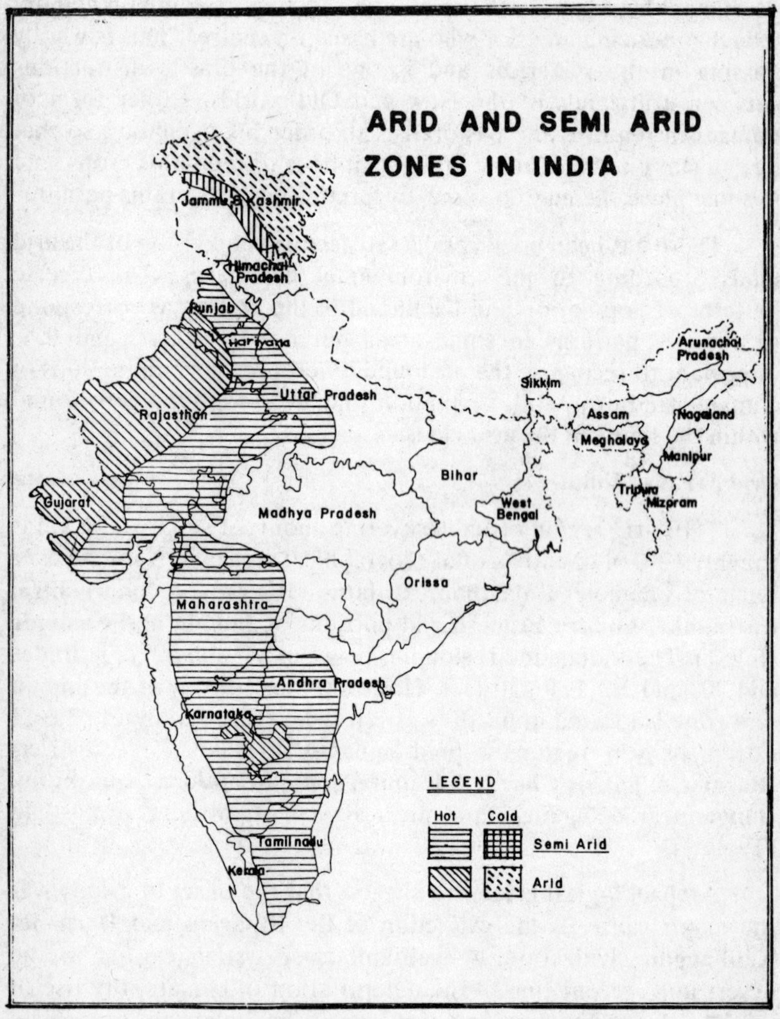

Fig. 1

Source : Govt. of India, Ministry of Agriculture, Deptt. of Agri. & Coop., New Delhi.

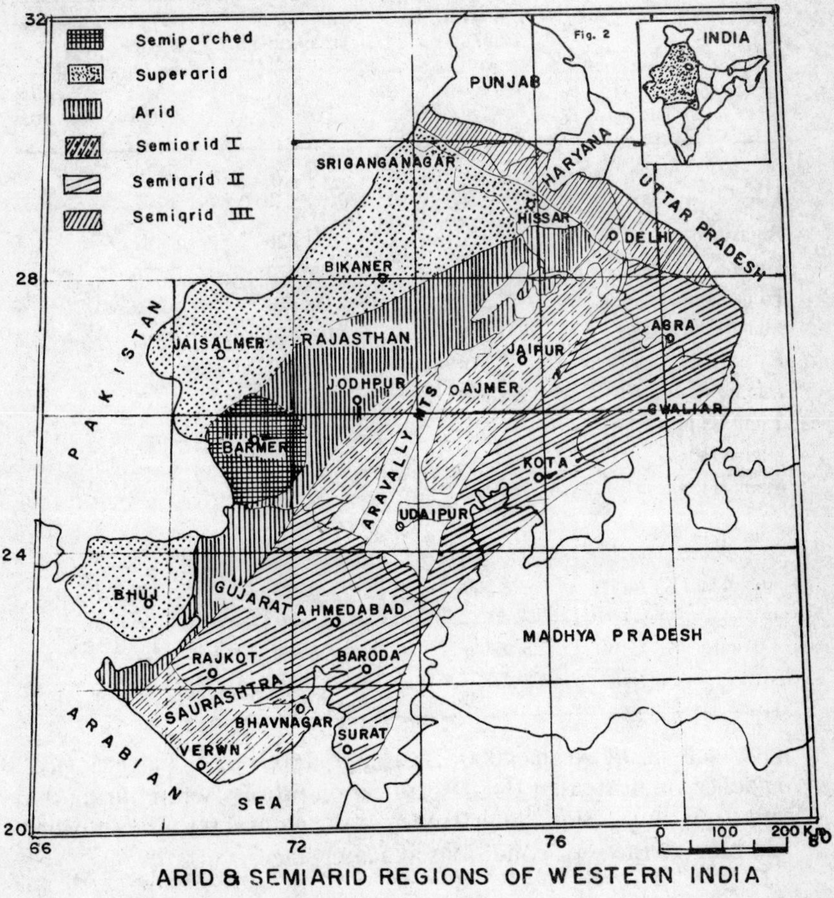
Semiparched
Superarid
Arid
Semiarid I
Semiarid II
Semiarid III
Fig. 2
INDIA
PUNJAB
HARYANA
UTTAR PRADESH
SRIGANGANAGAR
HISSAR
DELHI
BIKANER
PAKISTAN
JAISALMER
RAJASTHAN
JAIPUR
AGRA
JODHPUR
AJMER
GWALIAR
BARMER
ARAVALLY MTS
KOTA
UDAIPUR
BHUJ
GUJARAT
AHMEDABAD
MADHYA PRADESH
RAJKOT
BARODA
SAURASHTRA
BHAVNAGAR
SURAT
VERWN
ARABIAN
SEA
32
28
24
20
66
72
76
80
0
100
200 Km
ARID & SEMIARID REGIONS OF WESTERN INDIA

Fig. 2

Table-1 : State-wise distribution of arid and semi-arid areas in India

State	Arid area (km^2)	Semi-arid area (km^2)	Per cent distribution	
			Arid area	Semi-arid area
Hot				
Rajasthan	196.150	121.020	61	13
Gujarat	62.180	90.520	20	9
Punjab and Haryana	27.350	58.650	9	6
Maharashtra	1.290	189.580	Neg.	19
Karnataka	8.570	139.360	3	15
Andhra Pradesh	21.550	138.670	7	15
Tamil Nadu	—	95.250	—	10
Uttar Pradesh	—	64.230	—	7
Madhya Pradesh	—	59.470	—	6
Cold				
Jammu and Kashmir	78.300	13.780	—	—
Total	387.390	970.530	—	—
Total area of India	3,282.016	—	12	30

have set in between 4000 B.C. and 1000 B.C. Palynological evidences indicate that the desertification process set in during the late Cretaceous. Biotic interference of the natural resources further accentuated the xeric conditions at a later stage.

There are archaeological evidences to suggest that **Rajasthan, Punjab** and **Gujarat** were inhabited by man during the Palaeolithic period. Hand-axes made of quartzite have been found from **Jaipur** and **Indargarh**. These tools must be at least 2,00,000 years old.[5] **Misra and Rajaguru**[6] consider that the Middle Palaeolithic culture of the **Luni** Valley of the **Rajasthan** desert is of late Pleistocene age. There is considerable evidence that **Rajasthan** was inhabited by man early in Holocene times, though it is not certain whether there was cultural continuity from Palaeolithic to this Mesolithic period (c.f. Tilwara; 70° 5'E, 25° 52'N) estimated roughly to 5000 B.C. The **Harappan** culture has been traced at **Kalibangan,** situated on the bank of the 'lost' **Saraswati** river. Radio-carbon dating indicates that this culture flourished around 2700 B.C.[7] **Harappan** culture is generally placed at 2300-1750 B.C. More than a hundred sites of this culture have been discovered in the **Ghaggar** bed in the northern desert.

Semi-arid and arid zones are climatic classifications primarily based on indices of atmospheric moisture and these are essentially water deficit zones (Table - 2). Those regions where only two-third of the total water need of the region is met are semiarid and where only one-third of total water need is met are arid zones. The semiarid zones constitute 30.56% of total land area of India (Table 3) and are spread over 10 states (Table 4). Over 70% the semiarid area is confined to the southern states and the remaining 30% lies in the western part of the north-western states. The arid zones have comparatively less (one-third of semi-arid zones) coverage i.e. 10% the land area of India, and are largely confined to western states viz. 61% of total arid zones in Rajasthan state alone and 20% in Gujarat (Table 5).

Table-2 : Climatic classification(Adapted from Waite and Mather 1955)

Climatic Type	Code	Moisture Index (Im)	Moisture availability Index (MAI)
Humid (Per humid)	A	100	1.00
Sub-humid (Humid)	B	20 to 100	0.75-0.99
Moist (Moist sub-humid)	C	0 to 20	0.50-0.74
Sub-moist (Dry sub-humid)	D	0 to 33.3	0.25-0.49
Semi-arid Arid (Dry)	E	66.7 to 33.3 100.00 to 66.7	0.00-0.24

$$Im = \frac{[WS-WD] \times 100}{PE}$$

WS = annual water surplus
WD = annual water deficit
PE = annual water need

$$MAI = \frac{AE}{PE}$$

AE = actual evapotranspiration
PE = actual evapotranspiration

Table-3 : Climatic Zones of India

Zones	Lakh Km^2 Area	Per Cent
Humid	18.70	59.68
Semi-arid	9.56	30.56
Arid	3.18	10.16
Cold desert	0.84	0.03

*1 lakh = 100.000

Table-4 : Semiarid Zones of India

States	Lakh Km^2 Area	Per cent
Maharashtra	1.89	19.82
Karnataka	1.39	14.57
Andhra Pradesh	1.38	14.49
Rajasthan	1.21	12.64
Tamil Nadu	0.95	9.95
Gujarat	0.90	9.47
Uttar Pradesh	0.64	6.72
Madhya Pradesh	0.59	6.22
Punjab	0.32	3.32
Haryana	0.27	2.80

Table-5 : Arid Zones of India

States	Lakh Km^2 Area	Per cent
Rajasthan	1.95	61.0
Gujarat	0.64	20.0
Punjab	0.16	5.0
Haryana	0.13	4.0
Andhra Pradesh	0.22	7.0
Karnataka	0.09	3.0
Maharashtra	0.01	0.4

The climatic conditions in the 32 m ha arid tract in western Rajasthan are very harsh (Table 6). Thornth-waite's moisture index (Im) at different locations in the arid western Rajasthan varied from 69 to 91 and the aridity index (ia) ranges between 68 and 78. Evaporation from free water surface varies between 6.22 mm and 13.7 mm per day during winter and summer months respectively and the monthly water balance at a typical site in the Thar desert is 169 mm in January, 408 mm in April, and 79 mm in August.[8] Considering the water availability period and the length of the growing season.

Table-6 : Distribution and extent of arid region of north-west India

State	District	Total area of dist.	Percent arid area	Annual rain-fall (mm)	Moisture Index		Climate
					Mean	CV	
Rajasthan	Barmer	28173	100	260	-84	10	Arid
	Bikaner	28850	100	297	-83	10	Arid
	Jodhpur	22178	100	373	-80	13	Arid
	Churu	16851	100	368	-77	12	Arid
	Ganganagar	20414	100	248	-86	7	Arid
	Jaisalmer	41674	100	189	-91	7	Arid

(Contd.)

Table 6 (*Contd.*)

State	District	Total area of dist.	Percent arid area	Annual rain-fall (mm)	Moisture Index Mean	Moisture Index CV	Climate
	Nagaur	17718	96	333	-80	11	Arid
	Jalore	10563	88	388	-77	14	Arid
	Jhun Jhunu	5427	69	397	-75	13	Arid
	Sikar	7749	65	470	-69	21	Arid
	Pali	12297	48	424	-75	15	Arid
Gujarat	Kutch	45612	100	340	-82	—	Arid
	Jamnagar	14125	8	471	-80	—	Arid
	Rajkot	11203	6	594	-70	—	Arid
	Surendra nagar	10488	29	597	-74	—	Arid
	Junagarh	10607	20	623	-51	—	Semiarid
	Banaskantha	12702	18	627	-60	—	-do-
	Mehsana	9027	7	609	-63	—	-do-
	Ahmedabad	8707	6	783	-53	—	-do-
Haryana	Hissar	6331	90	438	-73	—	Arid
	Mahendragarh	2983	9	—	—	—	

Aridity In North-western India

Most (90%) of the Indian arid zone is located in north-western India, and about 62% of the extremely arid zone is predominantly located in 11 districts of western Rajasthan, 19% in Gujarat and 9 per cent in Punjab and Haryana districts. It is thus evident that 90% of the arid zones in India are located in north-western states of India. The present study on socio-demographic and ecological aspects of pastoral nomadism is mainly based on the data collected from Western districts of Rajasthan. It would, thus, not be out of place to present here some of the locational and ecological characteristics of these two states.

Rajasthan

Rajasthan, a well known State of India, is situated on the north-western part of India. It is somewhat square shaped in area.

The State has an area of 3,41,732 Sq. Km. with a population of 4.39 crores (1991 census-provisional). It is surrounded by Pakistan on the west and north-west, Punjab and Uttar Pradesh on the north-east and east, and Madhya Pradesh and Gujarat on the south-east and south-west. Its position lies between northern latitutdes of 23° – 3 min. and 20° – 12 min. and eastern longitudes between 69° – 30 min. and 78° - 17 min.

The Aravali range which runs from south-west to north- east direction in the State divides it into two parts with its highest peak at Guru Sikhar which is 5,650 Ft. only.

The north-western part is almost entirely a vast expanse of desert. The south-eastern part on the contrary has a varied terrain of extensive hill ranges, fertile table-lands and dense forests. The Chambal river and its tributary and the Banas, are the two large rivers of importance, other small rivers are the Lohi, Kali, Parvati, Mahir, etc.

The Tropic of Cancer passes through the southern part of Rajasthan and as is usually with the deserts of all continents, the Rajasthan desert lies above it. It has an extreme climate with very hot summers and cold winters, and very little amount of rainfall.

The average annual rainfall of the region varies from 150 to 500 mm with a coefficient of variation as high as 60-70 per cent (Fig. 3). The distribution of rainfall is also erratic, occurring mostly in the period july to September. During summer, the mean daily maximum temperature is generally 40°C and 22 to 28°C during winter. The mean minimum temperature varies from 24 to 26°C during summer and 4 to 10 C during winter. The mean relative humidity during summer varies from 36 to 50 per cent and from 66 to 78 per cent during monsoon during the morning hours.

The topography of Western Rajasthan is not a result of superficial or biogenic agencies, but is attributed to geological processes largely in the nature of the sheet movements leading to peneplanation, rapid changes in the drainage system, enormous accumulation of loose rocky materials, deepening of water-table and consequent depletion of vegetation, and thereby accentuation of desertic conditions.

Most spectacular amongst the land-forms are the dunes. These are present in 58 per cent area of the region. Within this, in nearly

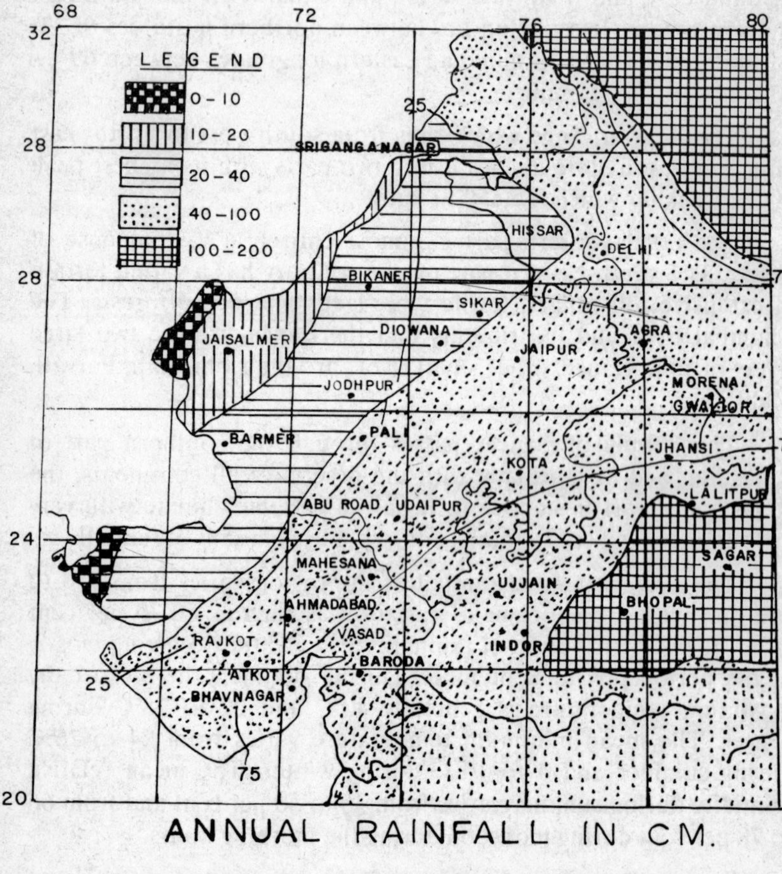

ANNUAL RAINFALL IN CM.

Fig. 3

30 per cent of the area dunes proper cover 60 to 100 per cent of the area, in 58 per cent these constitute 20 to 60 per cent of the area. The area of occurrence of dunes lies in the northern and western half of the region but even here it is not a contiguous feature and does have interludes of dune-free corridors such as the area from Pokran through Bap to Bikaner. A variety of dune formations such as coalesced parabolic, longitudinal, transverse, barchan and obstacle have been recognised.

The Central and Southern part of the arid Rajasthan is made up of medium and fine textured soil developed in situ or from alluvial parent material. These soils, as also those of dunes and sandy plains, are derived from alluvial parent material. The region is almost devoid of any signs of deflation or of aeolian sand. These soils have low nitrogen, but it is not a limitation in establishment and maintenance of good vegetation cover. Biogeographically, the majority of the desert biota exhibit Saharo-Rajasthani affinities as opposed to middle-Asian.

On the basis of physical features, the State can be divided into four broad regions viz., desert, hilly, plain and plateau.

(i) The Western Desert Region includes the districts of Barmer, Jalore, Jaisalmer, Jodhpur, Bikaner, Churu, Ganganagar, Nagaur and Pali. Agro-climatically, it is not suitable for crop-farming chiefly because of the lack of water.

(ii) **The Southern Hilly Region** comprises the districts of Banswara, Dungarpur, Udaipur and Sirohi.

(iii) **The South-Eastern Plateau Region** is formed of Kota, Bundi, Jhalawar, and Chittorgarh and Ajmer districts.

(iv) **The North-Eastern Plain Region** is composed of Alwar, Bharatpur, Jaipur, Jhunjhunu, Sikar, Swai-Madhopur, Bhilwara and Tonk districts.

Famines of different kinds namely **Akal**(great famine), **Jalkal** (Scarcity of water), **Tinkal** (Scarecity of fodder) and **Trikal** (Scarecity of fodder, water and grain), have been of common occurrence in the western Rajasthan. The historical situations revealed in a common traditional folk saying summarizing the expectation of periods of harsh conditions :

"7 Akal, 27 Zamana, 63 Kuria Kacha and 3 Bheesan Akal"

(In a span of 100 years there would be seven famine years, twenty seven good years, sixty three years of average harvest and three extreme famine years).

The extent of degree of famine dispersion is further revealed in a famous Rajasthani local saying :

"Pug Poongal, Sar Merte, Udraj Bikaner, Bhoolo Chukyo Jodhpur, Thayo Jaisalmer".

(Famine keeps its legs standing in Poongal region in the heart of desert, head in Merta, stomach in Bikaner and may move to Jodhpur and stays for ever in their home- town of Jaisalmer).

This particular folk saying indicates that some areas of western Rajasthan are less prone to desertic conditions and some are more prone to extreme desertic conditions.[9]

Population Characteristics

Spread over an area of 208 thousand Sq. Kms. the Rajasthan arid zone (consisting of 11 districts of western Rajasthan) has a population of 13.40 millions (1981). The region has an average density of 64 persons per sq.km and is one of the most thickly populated deserts of the world. The growth rate of population (1901-1981) in the arid zone of Rajasthan (excluding Ganganagar district where the rise has been mainly due to immigration of population) was 249% as compared to the Rajasthan State (231%) and of the country as a whole (187%). Similarly, within the arid zone of Rajasthan the percentage increase in population during the period 1901-81 has been 279%, 262%, 219% in the region receiving annual rainfall of less than 12" (excluding Ganganagar district), between 12"-16" and above 16", respectively.[10] The percentages of literacy in the State are 24,36 for males and 11 for females. However, in rural areas, it is only 18 per cent for the general masses. Thus, rural population of the State is generally illiterate.

Over 80 per cent of the population inhabit rural areas. Approximately two-thirds of the total population constitutes the non-working class. Such high percentage of economically inactive population may largely be attributed to the high concentration of population in lower age groups. The occupation distribution of the working population revealed that cultivation and agricultural labour formed the main occupation of over three-fourth of the total workers. Another major occupation followed by the workers is the operation of household industries and manufacturing other than household industries. Trade, mining and other services formed the chief occupation of small percentage of earners only. Animal husbandry is, however, often followed as a subsidiary occupation by the majority of the households and in certain pockets (where the aridity index is relatively high), such as the Anupagarh-Pugal region, it formed the main occupation of over-two thirds of the total workers.

On the basis of main economic activity, 30.5 per cent of the total population consists of workers. The working population is composed of 49.9 per cent of the male and 9.3 per cent of the female population. In rural areas 51 per cent of the males and 11 per cent of the females constitute the working force. Out of the total workers in rural areas, 73 per cent are cultivators and 8 per cent are agricultural labourers. Thus, 81 per cent of the working population is mainly dependent on agriculture for its livelihood. It also indicates that only a small part of the adult females is participating in the economically productive work. Agriculture with its allied activities engages 80 per cent of the male and 89 per cent of the female workers in rural areas. Only 3 per cent of the workers have livestock rearing, forestry, fishing etc. as their main economic activity, although 89 per cent of the rural households possess livestock. It shows that animal husbandry is generally a subsidiary economic activity of the rural masses.

The villages in the arid zone have a heterogeneous caste composition and the village society enjoined upon each caste to perform certain functions which were inter-dependent and complementary to each other, thereby weaving the economic system into a single integrated unit. Traditional occupations formed the basis of caste distinctions and of the economic system and its consequent bonds of mutual obligations. On the basis of the traditional occupations, the castes in the villages may be grouped into five broad categories, viz. (1) Agricultural castes like Jats, Bishnois, Rajputs, etc. (2) Castes serving the needs of agriculturists, like Suthars, Lohars, Bambis etc. (3) Caste serving the needs of the community with regard to the socio-religious ceremonies like

Brahmins, Sads, Swamies, Sewaks, Dakots and Dadis, (4) Castes serving the other needs of the community like Nais, Darjis, Sonars, Khatris, Kumhars, and Sansis, and finally (5) Castes having animal husbandry as the major occupation, like Raikas and Muslim cattle breeders (Goperas, Kharla, Billoch, etc.).

Settlement and Housing

It is largely due to the distinct physical and cultural characteristics of the desert, like the duny character of the landscape,, the scattered location of water sources, the socio-cultural heritage of certain castes, the **Jagirdari** system and the traditional custom of bringing in tenant- cultivators, that the majority, of the villages have either only scattered homesteads or have both compact and scattered homesteads. The society being patrilenial and patrilocal, the agnatic ties have much greater influence on the proximity of settlements. People living in scattered homesteads (dhanis) have greater economic advantages of close and continuous contact with the land, while the people living in scattered compact settlements at the core enjoy a richer social life. The nature of activities and type of social relationships of the people have been conditioned by the form of the settlement. The web of social relationships is confined within the cluster of **dhanis.** Households living at the core make greater use of the community facilities, while those living in the **dhanis** are inadequately covered. There is much smaller use of community facilities and the network of services such as education and health care normally do not reach the **dhanis.**

Resource Utilisation in Western Rajasthan

Human population has been living in balance with natural environment in the arid zone of India since centuries — balance being maintained sometimes by nature and at others by the adjustment mechanisms adopted by the desert inhabitants. History has it on record that man not only lived in this desert since ancient times but great civilizations flourished in the region.

The sources of livelihood and the way of life of the people have however been conditioned by the disturbance in the ecological balance owing to the severity of the arid climate, the continuous deterioration of the soil, the dwindling of natural resources, occasional drought, invasions by outsiders, poor means of communication and consequential social and economic uncertainties.

To cope up with such unfriendly climatic and environmental conditions, the inhabitants had evolved the socio-cultural means and mechanisms to live in balance with nature. The traditional social fabric among desert dwellers of western Rajasthan covering both the nomadic and sedentary population had created one integrated unit and provided for a judicious use of the fragile eco-system. The division of society according to their functional specialization, exchange relationships, water harvesting and its judicious use among the nomads, distinct settlement pattern, food habits, practice of agro-forestry, mixed farming, sequential farming, fallowing, the practice of **Khadin** cultivation herding a mixture of livestock with inbuilt socio-religious customs for preserving vegetation highlight the fact that inherent in the socio-economic system of the region were these tenacious means and adjustment mechanisms to cope with the hazardous and challenging situations and for maintaining the resource use equilibrium.

Resource use being the decisive factor of the pattern of their living, the population of Rajasthan's arid zone is divided into two major groups, viz., the nomadic and the sedentary. The pastoral nomads inhabited the extreme arid areas considered unsuitable for cultivation and engaged themselves in animal husbandry, supplying livestock and livestock products to the sedentary population (which inhabited slightly better areas permitting cultivation of cereal and non-cereal crops) in exchange for the cereal foods that were produced mainly by the agricultural castes. The other types of nomads also catered to the needs of the sedentary population in return for grains. The sedentary population by and large, lived in villages which were self- sufficient units except for the materials supplied by the nomads operating in the region.

Since the rainfall would not only vary five to ten folds from one year to another, but also during the same year at places just at a few km. from each other, the farmers were never sure of harvesting the grains. Most of them had subsidiary occupation like livestock raising which at least, ensured their survival. The livestock would also be able to survive on the fodder stalks that might be available in the event of no or partial harvest of grains. Again, as mentioned in the case of the nomads, the livestock raisers among the sedentary population also used to resort to migration to better rainfall areas which provided for their livestock and met their needs for survival.

The size of land held with the individual households were quite large and was scattered far and wide within several fragments in the boundary of the village. The farmers were generally of the opinion that greater number of fragments of land provided surety for getting some harvest from some plots as they may get rains while others may remain absolutely dry due to the erratic nature of the rainfall.

The above system thus had an in-built provision of leaving the lands fallow during the period these did not get rain. Even otherwise also, the farmers had developed the practice of leaving the land fallow after 4-5 years of its cultivation. This resulted in the land regaining fertility. The fallow lands also provided grazing resources for the livestock which, in turn, provided manure to these fields.[11]

Livestock Farming in Western Rajasthan

One of the most striking features of the lands in the 11 desert districts of Western Rajasthan is its lack of tangibility. Western Rajasthan which accounts for a major portion (62%) of the desertic lands presents both - exogenous as well as endogenous constraints which restricts their use - manoeuvarability. These constraints can be classified into three major categories viz., climatic, soil and the utilization constraints. These factors generate an extremely fragile eco-balance.

Agriculture in arid areas had its natural climatic limitations. The amount of rainfall is not necessarily low but varies widely from year to year and is very uncertain. This makes any agricultural activity, including grazing, extremely risky and insecure, and precludes the possibility of farming in small units.

Under such conditions, animal husbandry was and still remains the most important form of land use in the arid zones. Agro-climatic structure of western Rajasthan or arid zone of Rajasthan renders livestock and animal husbandry specially significant in the cast of land-use of Arid Zone of Rajasthan. In the arid zone climate is dry, the physiography is characterized either by sandy or rocky desert, dune and interdune sandy terrains, saline flat and depressions or playas (locally known as **rann**), sparsely populated and single cropped land. In this region therefore, animal husbandry is not merely an adjunct to agricultural operations, but supplementary avocation for the peasantry. In short, livestock farming has traditionally been one of the most viable elements of the agro-economic system of the arid zone of Rajasthan.

Livestock is an important asset of the arid zone of Rajasthan. Next to agriculture, it supplements households economy. With about 50 million heads of livestock, Rajasthan ranks third in India in animal wealth. More than eleven per cent of the total milk produced in the country is produced in Rajasthan. The State accounts for more than 50 per cent of the total national wool production, and is one of the principal suppliers of meat, egg and milk to the adjoining States. It also provides sturdy draught animals to the country. Since more than 60 per cent of the livestock of the State is concentrated in the arid areas of the State, these regions provide a major share of livestock production of the State.

Nomadic Pastoralism in Western Rajasthan

Among the many, well-defined and widely spread sectors of economic production in India is the multi-faceted 'industry' based upon livestock. There are caste (Jati) as well as tribal(Jana) groups - often called 'herding groups' - traditionally concerned with raising livestock and domesticating animals of several predominant species. Essentially an indigenous 'industry', it has evolved its own optimally suitable methods for upbringing locally available genetic stocks in the given eco-niches.

There are nearly thirty pastoral communities in India (Fig. 4). They are located particularly in the northern and Western parts of the country covering the states of Jammu & Kashmir, Himachal Pradesh, Uttar Pradesh, Haryana, Rajasthan and Gujarat. These are also found, though in relatively less concentration, in south covering States of Andhra Pradesh, Karnataka and Tamil Nadu. In other States, viz. Maharashtra and Madhya Pradesh, only a few communities have been noticed.

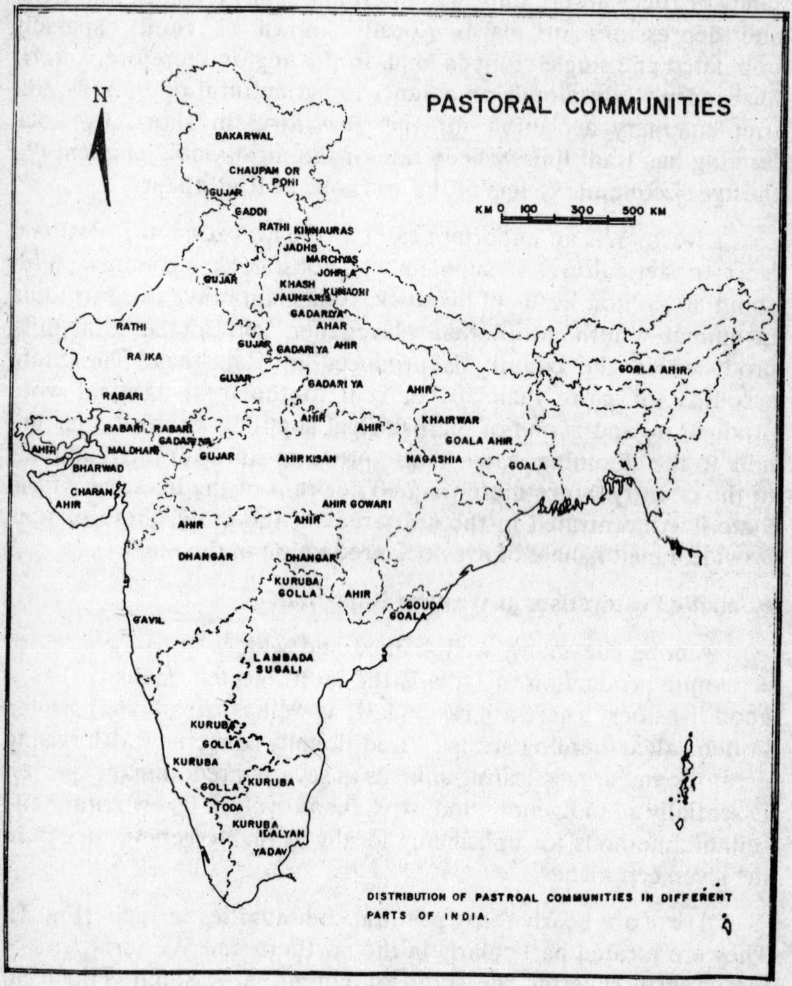

Fig. 4

Source : IGFRI, Jhansi

Pastoralism is an ecologically appropriate techniq-e in the Indian landscape, which substantially consists of arid, forest and mountanious areas where agriculture occupies a marginal place. It is estimated that in India there are 50 million livestock and 34 million people managing it. The groups concerned with livestock production may be divided into two categories :

1) There are groups in which livestock population is a predominant activity, such as the **Raikas** and **Sindhi Muslims** of Western Rajasthan; the **Rabaris** of Kuchch, Jamnagar and Kathiawad (Gujarat); the **Gaddis** of Himachal Pradesh; the **Gujars** (and **Bakarwal Gujars**) of Kashmir and Garhwal regions; and a number of shepherd castes of the Deccan plain and south India.

2) There are other groups predominantly engaged in agricultural activity, but significant elements of pastoralism enter into their mode of production, such as the **Bhatti Rajputs** of Jaisalmer; the **Bishnois** of Bikaner and Sri Ganga Nagar; the **Jats, Rajputs** and **Ahirs** of Rajasthan as a whole, and many other parts throughout the country.

Pastoral occupations involve nomadism to a certain extent as animals soon eat up the grass and have to be moved to new areas. Deficient rainfall, and scarcity of water during dry periods also necessiate their migration to more favourable areas. The movement is often rendered necessary as a result of fouling of the ground by the animals, or out- breaks of contagious diseases. Pastoralism, therefore, came to be developed as a distinct occupation, requiring specialised knowledge and experience of herd management, grazing areas and grasses, and the availability of grazings and water in different tracts during different seasons.

Though pastoralism is differentially associated with nomadic existence, on the whole the pastoral groups in India have their 'permanent villages' and those who go on grazing expeditions return to their villages after eight or nine months. Compared to these regular migrant groups, the irregular nomadic people are settled flock-owners and indulge in pastoralism to supplement agriculture. They may be on a short-term migration in lean periods of drought and hunger when there is an acute shortage of fodder.

The traditional systems of economic production, such as agriculture and pastoralism, had been well integrated and synergistic. But with technological changes and reclamation of land for agricultural and other developmental purposes, this synergism is adversely affected. With changes in the modes of production, infusion of foreign technology and demographic pressure on land, the pastoral groups are experiencing grave consequences of impoverishment and proletarianization. It is my conviction that the demographic reality of India is inconceivable without its livestock: the milk of cow and buffalo, the traction power of bullock and dromedary, the wool of sheep, goat and camel, and the skin of these animals, are essential aspects of economic production. And, therefore, a discussion of livestock elements and the traditional specialists concerned with production is indispensable not only for an economic-oriented consideration but also for understanding rural development in India.

The arid lands are most vulnerable to desertification. Desertification in broad sense means deterioration of land, water, vegetation and other natural resources under ecological stress. Deterioration may be due to natural or human activities with an objective to maximise short-term gain at the expense of long-term productivity. Animal-human activity in the Indian desert has revealed that ecological deterioration and accentuation of desertification has been occuring in the region in recent times due to the intense human and livestock pressure. The increased pressure of livestock on the natural grazing lands has resulted in over exploitation of resources leading to depletion of natural vegetation.

The impact of animal-human relationship on desertification at global level has been viewed from various angles. Most of these studies have also correlated desertification with the social, economic, bio-physical and environmental factors connected with landscape changes, vegetational degradation, loss of livelihood, pastures turning into waste lands, decrease in crop productivity, etc.

A particularly important area of neglect is the livestock population, ecology and behaviour of domesticated animals in relation to the vegetation on the one hand and the cultural strategies on the other. Therefore, socio- economic, cultural and environmental factors of pastoral nomadism are of great importance.

The system of land-use evolved by animal husbandmen in arid zones, and more particularly by pastoral nomads, in response to the major agro-climatic factors, have themselves induced further desiccation caused by excessive removal of the vegetation. These man-induced types of desiccation may themselves have led to major migrations of the pastoralists.

It has been widely recognized that the crucial problem of Indian arid zone is a growing imbalance between population pressure and declining land productivity. It is also widely believed, but not appreciated enough, that physical deterioration of resource base is, to a large extent, conditioned by socio-economic structure of increasing population. The settled and nomadic populations, which in past provided checks against excessive resource exploitation mainly through traditional and less intensive landuse and hence maintained an ecological equilibrium. With the passage of time, the increased population growth is leading to a break-down in traditional relationships which has made nomadic pastoralism an extremely difficult avocation to be maintained in the arid environment.

REFERENCES

1. Hills, E.S 1969. Arid Lands in Geographical Appraisal (edited) **Methuen & Co. Ltd.**, Paris. UNESCO.
2. Ibid.
3. Wadia, D.N. 1960. The Past Glacial Descication of Central Asia. **Mongr. natn. Inst. Sci India** 10 : 1-25.
4. Krishnan, M.S. 1952. Geological History of Rajasthan and to Present Day Conditions. **Bull. natn. inst. India** 1: 19-31.
5. Sankhalia, H.D. 1952. The condition of Rajputana in the past as deduced from Archaeological evidence. **Proe. Symp. Rajasthan Desert. Bull. natn. Inst. Sci. India** 43-49.
6. Misra, V.N. and Rajguru, S.N. 1976. Some Aspects of Quaternary Environment and Early Man In Western India. **Workshop on the Problems of Desert in India**, Jaipur.
7. Prakash, Satya. 1964. Archaeology. Recent Developments in Rajasthan. **Souvenir Vol. CAZRI**, Jodhpur, 134-138.
8. Ray, S.B. 1985. Soil Water Plant Atmosphere Relationship : In Singh, S.D (ed.). **Irrigated Agriculture in Arid Areas** WAPCOS, New Delhi 417 pp.
9. Malhotra, S.P. 1988. Man and the Desert. In **Desert Ecology**(ed.) Scientific Publishers, Jodhpur. p.37-64.
10. Ibid.
11. Ibid.
12. Randhawa, M.S. 1959. Farmers of India. **ICAR**, New Delhi

3

Increasing Population Pressure and Pastoral Nomadism

Long before history began, animals had been domesticated, and represented an important part of the economic structure and had a significant effect on the social systems of primitive societies. Animal husbandry was and still remain the most important form of land use in the semi-arid and arid zones of the Old World.[1]

The livestock industries of arid and semi-arid zones are carried on within the limits imposed by an environment composed of the usual factors of climate, soil and vegetation. These general characteristics are also related to the geology and geomorphology of the site. The most important factors influenencing the present nature and extent of a livestock industry and the degree to which it can be improved are, however, biotic in nature. The actual existence of man and his grazing and browsing animals in arid and semi-arid zones affects not only these habitats themselves, but also extends the area of aridity into zones which were not originally of this type. The degeneration of vegetation, however, is due as much to man's need for land for cultivation as to overgrazing. The men who live with and by livestock in arid zones are also an important, if not the dominant factor of the total environment or biome.

Owing to the increasing pressure of population on the limited cultivable land available, the land use pattern in the arid areas has witnessed phenomenal change. The system of land use evolved, by animal husbandmen in arid zones, and more particularly by the nomads, in response to the major changes in climate, have according to most authorities, themselves, induced further desiccation caused by excessive removal of the vegetative cover.[2] These man-induced types of desiccation have led to increase in the pastoral nomadism.

Socio-economic surveys and agro-economic investigations of both settled and nomadic populations have identified social and economic elements which in past provided checks against excessive resource exploitation mainly through traditional and less intensive land use and hence maintained an ecological equilibrium. With the passage of time, the increased population growth led to break down in traditional relationships which may have contributed to the present imbalance. One of the greatest calamities borne out of this process has been irrational use of land which accentuates resource degradation and consequently helps setting in motion forces of desertification.[3]

The arid zone society in the past has been frequently exposed to high mortality rate. Thus social structure not only permitted but encouraged higher fertility rates in human population. Actually there is an overwhelming evidence of built in high fertility norms and preference for sons which has led to larger human population base. Arid Rajasthan has an even higher growth rate than Rajasthan as a whole, and Rajasthan has a higher rate than the whole of India. Malhotra[4] has enumerated high fertility norms originally developed in high mortality conditions,considerations of lineage, social values and the sharp decline in mortality as the factors responsible for this extraordinary growth rate.

The human population of Rajasthan increased 33 per cent between 1971 and 1981 and this is a continuation of an ongoing expansion (Tables 7 to 9). The desert Districts of Barmer, Jodhpur and Jaissalmer increased in population over the last decade 44%, 45% and 45% respectively. Taking a longer view, in Jodhpur District, the population increased fourfold between 1901 and 1981, from 400,000 to 1,700,000. The overall population density in Rajasthan is 100 persons per square kilometre, Jodhpur district having a density of 73 persons per sq.km. The rural population density of Jodhpur District jumped from 34 sq.km. in 1971 to 48 per sq.km. in 1981.[5] The last few decades have seen an unprecedented

Table – 7: Decadal Variation in Total Population of Rajasthan and Three Western Desert Districts*

Rajasthan Year	Persons	Percentage decade variation	Jaisalmer		Jodhpur		Barmer	
1901	10,294,090	-	75,551	-	424,461		313.102	
1911	10,983,509	+6.70	87,162	+15.37	434,954	+2.47	299,518	-4.34
1921	10,292,648	-6.29	69,224	-20.58	382,545	+12.05	281,438	-6.04
1931	11,747,974	+14.14	78,646	-13.61	443,654	+15.97	308,264	- 9.53
1941	13,863,859	+18.01	96,958	+23.28	558,389	+25.86	394,529	+27.98
1951	15,970,774	+15.20	109,658	+13.10	672,109	+20.37	477,282	+20.98
1961	20,155,602	+26.20	141,242	+28.20	884,759	+31.64	649,794	+36.14
1971	25,765,806	+27.83	167,824	+18.82	1,151,649	+30.17	774,805	+19.24
1981	34,261,862	+32.97	243,082	+44.82	1,667,791	+44.82	1,118,892	+44.41

*Adapted from CENSUS OF INDIA 1981, Series 18, RAJASTHAN, Part II-A, General Population Tables, Jaiplur, 1983, pp. 166, 168.

Table – 8 : Decadal Variation In Rural Population Of Rajasthan And Three Western Desert Districts*

State/District	1981	1971	1961	1951	1941	1931	1921	1911	1901
Rajasthan	27,051,354	21,222,045	16,874,124	13,015,499	11,746,758	10,018,769	8,817,313	9,507,680	8,743,434
Jaisalmer	210,155	143,477	127,596	96,515	85,290	67,010	59,956	73,928	61,289
Jodhpur	1,087,946	783,411	619,549	448,839	390,050	313,513	278,743	320,397	310,620
Barmer	1,020,663	718,580	610,084	444,515	327,535	292,009	267,476	285,572	298,720

*Adapted from CENSUS OF INDIA 1981, Series 18, RAJASTHAN, Part II-A, General Population Tables, Jaipur, 1983, p.90

Table – 9 : Percentage of Population Increase By State In 1961 - 71 and 1971 - 81

		1961-71		1971-81
Gujarat		29.3		27.21
Maharashtra		27.3		24.36
Madhya Pradesh		28.7		25.15
Karnataka		24.1		26.43
*Rajasthan	rank no. 3	27.6	rank no. 1	32.36
Orissa		25.0		19.72
Uttar Pradesh		19.8		25.49
Punjab		21.0		23.01
Bihar		21.2		23.90
Andhra Pradesh		20.6		22.76
Tamil Nadu		22.0		17.23

* Adapted from INDIA's CHANGING RURAL SCENE 1963-1979, Gilbert Etienne, Delhi : O.U.P., 1982, p.147.

rise in the population pressure i.e. from 17.2 persons per square kilometre in the year 1921 to 30.0 in 1961 and 68.4 in 1981 (Fig. 5).[6]

The best demographic data presently known for Rajasthan from late mediaeval period are from **Mahnot Nainsi,** a chief revenue official of **Raja Jaswant Singh** who ruled **Marwar** State(which was roughly equivalent to the present day districts of **Jodhpur, Nagaur, Jalor** and **Pali**) from 1638 to 1681. Nainsi during the period 1658 -1662 traversed **Marwar** State and made a detailed record of, among other things, the location of villages, the number of households, ponds, wells, and the type and size of crop. These data allow an estimate of the population.Table 10 shows such an estimate for some villages in the **Phalodi** area of Jodhpur district.

The results show a vartiation in size of village similar to the present, from 72 to 2432. More importantly the population in most villages was appreciably less than the present. The population of all the villages together recorded for 1658-1662 is less than half the mean for the census years 1891,1921 and 1941. Thus, over a period

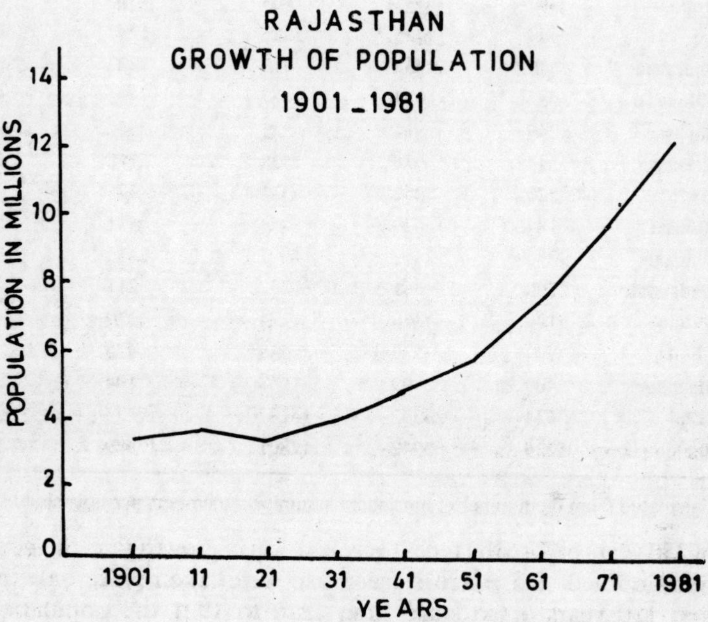

Fig. 5

Source : R.P. Dhir, 1988 (See References).

Table – 10 : Population Growth In Selected Villages of Phalodi Area.

Village name	Census year 1660	1891	1921	1941	1971
Lohawat	2432	5366	4663	5537	9855
Naneo	72	898	451	565	1459
Sanwriji	1200	957	623	1094	2449
Hopali	440	432	503	610	1062
Au	648	2721	1555	1797	2789
Bheeyasar	640	1533	818	823	1196
Mungasar	488	1039	627	791	1518
Banasar	240	814	521	562	1035
Kelausar	344	976	528	790	1685
Jaislo	520	852	631	975	2173
Ranisar	184	629	458	411	813
Khichan	376	2449	1977	2658	2795
Dadarwalo	200	661	252	211	502
Mithio	120	356	174	119	231
Chhila	320	530	438	428	816
Mayakor	400	99	68	104	251
Total	8624	23312	14287	17475	30629
Phalodi Town	5226	3942	12801	17689	17379

Calculated from the number of household assuming 8 members per household.

of 250 years before the recent acceleration in growth rate, the population doubled. This increase seems to have taken place only in the first 150 years or so since from 1820 to 1921 the population of Marwar State as a whole seems to have remained around two million.

A process of phenomenal growth seems to have set in from 1921 onwards, as is shown by the figures of subsequent censuses for **Jodhpur** district and for the area of erstwhile **Marwar** State, in Fig 6. The population almost doubled in the forty-year period from 1921 to 1961 and then increased further 30% in just a decade. This growth seems to be in conformity with the trend in the larger region[7] (see Table 11).

The bulk of the population base in 1961 (Table 12) came from **Ganganagar, Nagaur, Pali, Sikar and Barmer** districts of arid

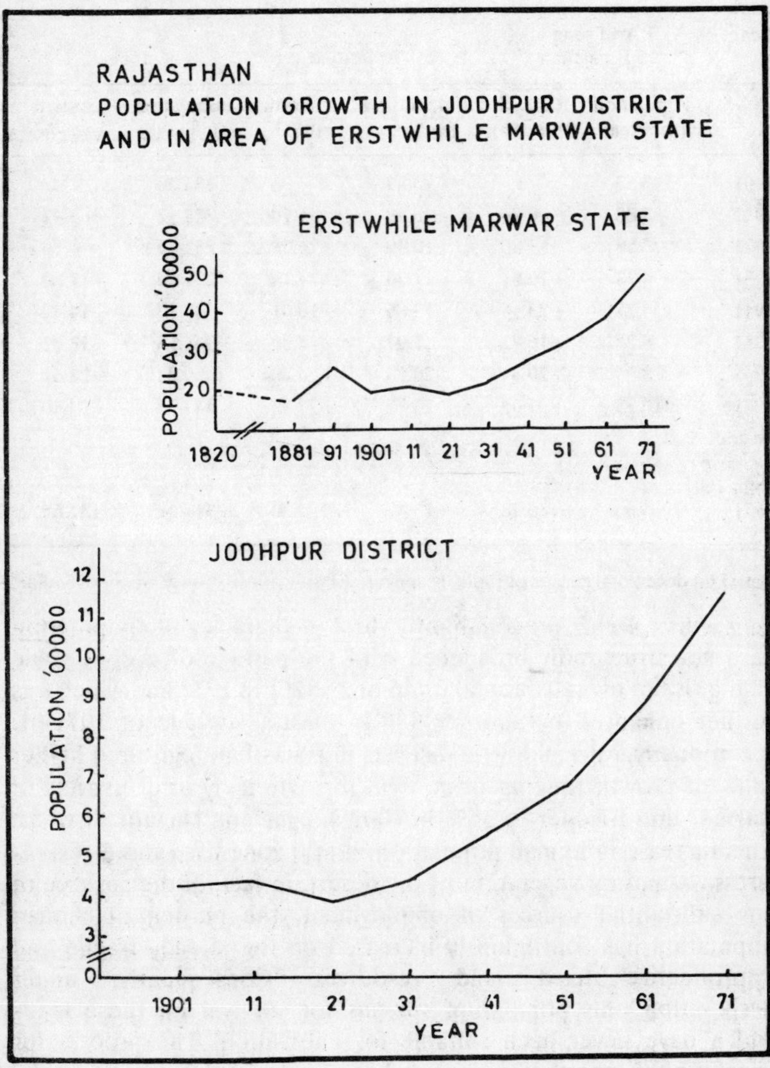

Fig. 6

Source : R.P. Dhir, 1982 (See References).

Table – 11 : Decennial Percent Variation in Population in Arid Zone of Rajasthan and India 1901 - 1971.

Year	Arid zone of Rajasthan		Rajasthan		India	
	Population (millions)	Growth rate(%)	Population (millions)	Growth rate(%)	Population (millions)	Growth rate(%)
1901	3.57		10.29		236.28	
1911	3.88	+8.70	10.98	+6.70	252.12	+5.42
1921	3.58	-7.80	10.29	-6.29	251.35	-0.303
1931	4.28	+19.81	11.75	+14.14	279.02	+11.00
1941	5.28	+23.16	13.86	+18.01	318.70	+14.22
1951	6.2	+16.73	15.97	+15.20	361.13	+13.31
1961	8.0	+29.84	20.16	+26.20	439.24	+21.64
1971	10.23	+27.95	25.77	+27.83	547.37	+24.66
Overall increase from 1901 1971	6.66	+186.78	+15.47	+150.30	+311.08	131.65

Based on deceminal census of India, Manager of Publications, Government of India.

Rajsasthan. Being predominantly rural in character the population base got structurally broadened with the passage of every decade giving rise to overall decadal jump of 28.31% in 1971 and which was further enhanced by another 9% in ensuing decade of 1971-81. Additionally, extremely arid districts in Rajasthan registered higher rates of growth ranging from 19% for extremely arid districts of **Barmer and Bikaner** to 35% in **Ganganagar and Nagaur** districts. This increase in human population in arid zone has caused serious stress on natural vegetation of the desert. In fact, in the absence of any substantial sources of employment, the burden of human population has continuously increased on the already fragile and unproductive fixed land resources. Consequently, under desperation, this population spreads for survival on those lands which have never been suitable for cultivation. The process for checking the population growth has also been slow owing to the characteristic social fabric of the society inhabiting arid region.

Table – 12: Human Population in Arid Districts of Western Rajasthan (in lakhs)*

District	1961			1971			1981			Decadal variation of total populaltion	
	Rural	Urban	Total	Rural	Urban	Total	Rural	Urban	Total	1961-71	1971-81
Barmer	6.10	0.39	6.49	7.18	0.50	7.74	10.20	0.98	11.18	19.26	44.44
Bikaner	2.56	1.80	4.44	3.35	2.37	5.72	5.13	3.35	8.48	28.82	48.25
Churu	4.50	2.08	6.58	6.15	2.58	8.73	8.34	11.78	32.44	34.93	34.93
Gangangar	8.87	1.49	10.36	11.64	2.29	13.93	16.11	4.18	20.29	34.45	45.65
Jaisalmer	1.26	0.13	1.39	1.42	0.24	1.66	2.10	0.33	2.43	19.42	46.38
Jalore	5.22	0.24	5.46	6.38	0.29	6.67	8.30	0.73	9.03	22.16	35.38
Jhunjhunu	5.92	1.27	7.19	7.67	1.62	9.29	9.60	2.51	12.11	29.16	30.35
Jodhpur	6.20	2.65	8.85	7.84	3.68	11.52	10.87	5.79	16.66	30.16	44.61
Nagaur	8.14	1.20	9.34	11.07	1.55	12.62	13.91	2.37	16.28	35.11	29.00
Pali	7.28	0.76	8.04	8.61	1.08	9.69	10.39	2.34	12.73	19.27	32.74
Sikar	6.76	1.43	8.19	8.65	1.77	10.42	10.98	2.78	13.76	27.22	32.05
	62.81	13.52	76.33	73.36	18.03	97.99	105.93	28.80	134.73	28.35	37.49

* Lakh = 100,000

The social factors are essentially a combination of attributes or conditions (viz. poverty, illiteracy), behaviours (preferance for large families), values and beliefes (sanctity of cows) and institutional arrangements.

The socio-demographic constraints result in the unequal distribution of assets and resultant consequences of unequal distribution of income, consumption and opportunities are too common to merit attention. Socio-demography in this region is also conditioned negatively by illiteracy and general lack of education in arid areas. Lack of communication and transport combine to make illiteracy of rural population a formidable constraints having far reaching consequences. Some of these consequencs have led to trends of yore of having built-in preferences for larger families in favour of fragmentation of households into small, nuclear ones. This tendency has led to the fast decline in land-man ratio, and has rendered the whole farming insensitive to size economics in the arid region.[8]

Livestock Population

Livestock population, like human population, has also increased tremendously in the last three decades in Western Rajasthan. In Rajasthan as a whole, the livestock population (mixed species) rose from 34 million in 1957 to almost 50 million in 1983, and there was an increase in livestock density from 99 per sq.km to 145 per sq.km (Table13). In the desert districts where sheep and goat predominate (over 70% of the total), the livestock numbers just about doubled between 1956 and 1983, from 800,000 to 1,500,000 to 3,500,000 in **Jodhpur.**

According to the livestock census report (1983), the eleven arid and semi-arid districts (Barmer, Bikaner, Churu, Ganganagar, Jaisalmer, Jalor, Jhunjhunu, Jodhpur, Nagaur, Pali and Sikar) comprising the Western Rajasthan part of the Thar, or the Great Indian desert harbour a total domestic livestock population of nearly 23.2 million heads - an increase of nearly 4.2 million heads over the 1977 census figures. The total livestock population of the State, as per the 1983 census being 49.5 million, the desert region may well have about 47 per cent, or nearly half of the State's livestock population.

Table – 13 : District – wise Livestock Area and Density

Districts		Total livestock as per 1983 Census (in lakhs)	Area (Sq.km)	Livestock density per Sq.Km (as per 1983 Census)
1.	Ajmer	19.86	8481	234
2.	Alwar	16.54	8380	197
3.	Banswara	10.25	5037	203
4.	Barmer	31.84	28387	112
5.	Bharatpur	9.92	5090	195
6.	Bhiwara	26.85	10455	257
7.	Bikaner	20.75	27244	76
8.	Bundi	9.68	5550	174
9.	Chittorgarh	18.45	10856	170
10.	Churu	21.30	16830	126
11.	Dholpur	4.54	3010	151
12.	Dungarpur	11.04	3770	293
13.	Ganganagar	21.85	20634	106
14.	Jaipur	31.11	14068	221
15.	Jaisalmer	16.31	38401	42
16.	Jalore	14.76	10640	139
17.	Jhalawar	10.03	6219	161
18.	Jhunjhunu	11.76	5928	198
19.	Jodhpur	26.66	22850	117
20.	Kota	14.89	12436	120
21.	Nagour	30.56	17718	172
22.	Pali	20.12	12387	162
23.	S.Madhopur	17.91	10527	170
24.	Sikar	17.59	7732	227
25.	Sirohi	7.62	5136	148
26.	Tonk	14.73	7194	206
27.	Udaipur	39.58	17279	229
	Rajasthan	496.50	342239	145

If we examine livestock census data pertaining to the desert districts of Rajasthan from the census year 1956 to the census year 1983 - a period covering 27 years - certain interesting facts emerge. During this period, cattle registered the lowest (23%) growth rate, sheep (81.%) and goat (86%) populations had very high growth rates while buffaloes have registered a strikingly high growth rate of 125 per cent (which is possibly more of an indication of increased availability of water in the region through canals and dug wells in recent times than anything else. The region thus, had 78% more livestock to feed in 1983 than in 1956. This staggering increase in animal numbers is also reflected in the quantum jump in the human : livestock ratio of 100:117 a decade back to that of 100:173. Within the desert region, there being nearly 13.4 million human beings in the 11 desert districts of Rajasthan, according to the 1981 census report. Incidentally, while the decennial - 1971 (10.2 million) - 1981 (13.4 million) - increase in human population in the arid zone of Rajasthan has been almost 31.3 per cent, the livestock population during the 11 year period 1972 (16.3 million) -1983 (23.2 million) increased by more than 42 per cent (table 14).

Table – 14 : Districtwise Population & Livestock Number & Their Ratio- Rajasthan

(In Lakhs)*

Districts		Total Population 1981	Livestock 1983	Ratio (Col. 2 & 3)
1		2	3	4
1.	Ajmer	14.40	19.86	1.38
2.	Alwar	17.71	16.55	0.93
3.	Banswara	8.87	10.27	1.16
4.	Barmer	11.19	31.04	2.85
5.	Bharatpur	12.99	9.92	0.76
6.	Bhiwara	13.10	26.84	2.04
7.	Bikaner	8.49	20.75	2.44
8.	Bundi	5.87	9.66	1.64
9.	Chittorgarh	12.32	18.46	1.49
10.	Churu	11.79	21.28	1.80
11.	Dholpur	5.85	4.55	0.78
12.	Dungarpur	6.83	11.05	1.61
13.	Ganganagar	20.30	21.86	1.07
14.	Jaipur	34.21	31.10	0.91

(*Contd.*)

1		2	3	4
15.	Jaisalmer	2.43	16.31	6.67
16.	Jalore	9.03	14.76	1.64
17.	Jhalawar	7.85	10.03	1.28
18.	Jhunjhunu	12.12	11.76	0.97
19.	Jodhpur	16.68	26.66	1.59
20.	Kota	15.60	14.87	0.95
21.	Nagour	16.29	30.35	1.87
22.	Pali	12.74	20.13	1.10
23.	S.Madhopur	15.36	17.92	1.30
24.	Sikar	13.77	17.60	1.24
25.	Sirohi	5.42	7.61	1.40
26.	Tonk	7.84	14.74	1.88
27.	Udaipur	23.57	39.58	1.70
	Rajasthan	342.62	496.50	1.45

*Lakh = 100,000

Growth of livestock population in the State during the last three decades is presented in Table 15. The general trend shows a declining ratio of livestock to human population since 1956. Composition of species also shows a marked change (Fig. 7). The share of cattle in total livestock has secularly declined, while that of goats and sheep has increased. Buffalo population has also increased at a faster rate than cattle population. The rapid growth of bovine population has adversely affected fodder resources, and has created many problems in the rural areas of Rajasthan.

Size and Composition of Bovine Population. In 1983, there were 19.5 million bovine animals in the State. The ratio of bovine to human poulation was 54 bovines for every 100 persons, which was higher than the corresponding national average of 38 in 1977. For every hundred hectares of cultivataed area, the State had 124 bovines. The density of bovine population was 57 animals per sq.km. By either index, the density of bovine population in the State is lower than the national averages of 150 and 72 respectively.

Table – 15 : Trends in Size and Composition of Livestock in Rajasthan

(Number in million)

Category	1951	1956	1961	1966	1972	1977	1983 (Provisional	%age Change during 1951-83	Annual Compound Growth Rate(%) 1951-77	1977-83
1. Cattle	10.77 (42.2)	12.07 (37.2)	13.14 (39.2)	13.12 (35.0)	12.47 (32.1)	12.90 (31.2)	13.47 (27.2)	+25	0.7	0.7
2. Buffaloes	3.05 (11.9)	3.44 (10.6)	4.02 (12.0)	4.22 (11.3)	4.59 (11.8)	5.07 (12.2)	6.03 (12.2)	+98	2.0	2.9
3. Sheep	5.39 (21.1)	7.37 (22.7)	7.36 (22.0)	8.81 (23.5)	8.56 (22.0)	9.94 (24.0)	13.39 (27.1)	+148	2.4	5.1
4. Goats	5.59 (31.9)	8.73 (27.0)	8.05 (24.0)	10.32 (27.5)	12.16 (31.3)	12.31 (29.8)	15.41 (31.1)	+176	3.1	3.9
5. Others	0.74 (2.9)	0.81 (2.5)	0.94 (2.8)	1.00 (2.7)	1.10 (2.8)	1.14 (2.8)	1.19 (2.4)	+61	1.7	0.7
Total Livestock	25.54 (100.0)	32.42 (100.0)	33.51 (100.0)	37.47 (100.0)	38.88 (100.0)	41.36 (100.0)	49.49 (100.0)	+94	1.8	3.0

(*Contd.*)

1	2	3	4	5	6	7	8	9	10	11
Livestock per 100 human Population	160	180	166	163	147	137	138			
Adult Female Bovines per 100 persons	35	34	35	30	27	25	23			

Source: (i) 19 years of Agriculture in Rajasthan, 1977.
(ii) Techno-Economic Survey of Rajasthan, 1963.
(iii) Basic Statistics, Rajasthan, 1983.

Note: Figures in parentheses indicate column percentages.

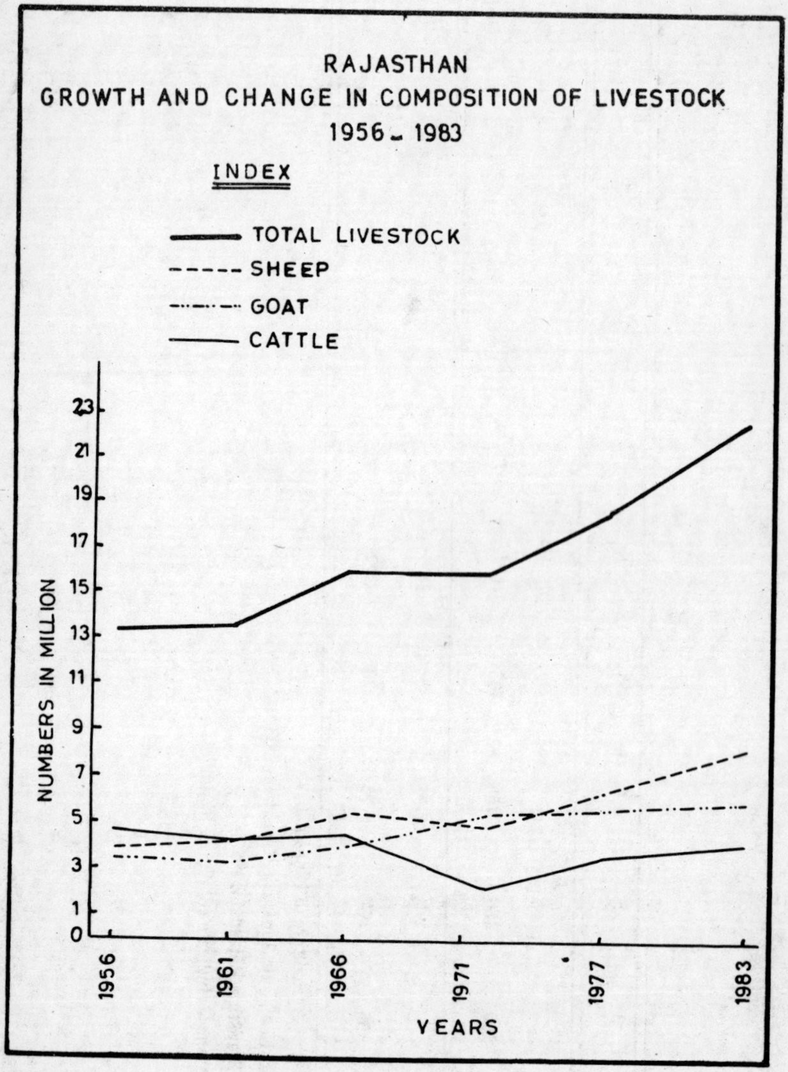

Fig. : 7

Source : R.P. Dhir, 1988 (See References).

Distribution of land in the State is highly skewed in favour of the big farmers. Next only to land the bovine animals constitute a very important and widely-held productive assets with the rural households of the State. The livestock assets constitute about 80 per cent of their total productive assets other than land. Bovine animals account for 62 per cent of the total value of assets. However, importance of bovines in asset holdings vary from region to region (Table 16).

Table – 16 : Share of Livestock in Total Value of Assets with the Rural Households in Rajasthan (1971-72)

Region	Percentage share of different assets (other than land)						
	Cattle	Buffalo	Bovine (2+3)	Other Live-stock	Total Live-stock (4+5)	Other Assets	Total Assets
Western	28.48	13.62	42.10	41.59	83.69	16.31	100.00
North-Eastern	40.75	23.73	64.48	10.71	75.19	24.81	100.00
Southern	51.77	24.88	76.65	7.74	84.39	15.61	100.00
South-Eastern	53.98	25.57	79.55	4.54	84.09	15.91	100.00
State	40.59	21.20	61.79	18.53	80.32	19.68	100.00

Source : Government of India, National Sample Survey, 26th Round, July 1971, September 1972, Report No. 215, State Tables - Rajasthan, Department of Statistics, New Delhi.

Notes: (i) Other assets include agricultural machinery, non-farm business equipment and transport equipment.

In the Southern and South-Eastern regions they constitute more than three-fourths of the total assets. In the Western Arid Region other livestock species are equally important.[9]

Livestock versus Human Population

Western Rajasthan stands out among physically similar regions of the world by virtue of the present high density of human and livestock population and of the long history of human settlement. Livestock rearing is the predominant. characteristics of the population inhabiting the dry region. Associated with it, animal-human relationship and its role in creating ecological imbalance is significant to a great extent in arid and semi-arid regions of the Indian sub- continent. Animal-human interactions, inter-relations, conditions and consequences constitute the components of constraints of maintaining a congruous and sustainable livestock economy in the desert ecology.

A study conducted by **Bharara,**[10] to examine the growth patterns of human and livestock population in different ecological regions of the arid zone of Rajasthan as compared to the Rajasthan State as whole, found that livestock per capita was higher in different ecological regions of arid Rajasthan (Table 17).Livestock was found to be associated with the extent of rainfall and aridity availability of grazing and fallow lands, traditional caste occupation and type of communities inhabiting the arid zone of Rajasthan. With the increase in aridity, due to less rainfall, there is increase in livestock favouring animal husbandry rather than cultivation. According to 1983 census, Livestock per capita was found to be minimum in **Jhunjhunu** (0.98) followed by **Ganganagar** (1.09), **Sikar** (1.28), **Pali** (1.58), **Jodhpur** (1.61), **Jalore** (1.63),**Churu** (1.74) and **Nagaur** (1.86); and maximum in **Jaisalmer** (6.76), followed by **Barmer** (2.85) and **Bikaner** (2.45). The later category of districts had lesser rainfall and higher aridity index and more grazing and fallow lands, as compared to the former category. Thus considerable increase in livestock population coupled with the human population revealed overstocked as well as over-peopled arid areas of Rajastan.

Table – 17 : Human versus Livestock Population

Area	Human Population No.	Human Population Period	Livestock Population No.	Livestock Population Period	Livestock/ Per capita (No.)
Rajasthan State	34.10 (million)	(1981)	49.48 (million)	(1983)	1.45
Rajasthan arid Zone	13.40 (million)	(1981)	23.21 (million)	(1983)	1.72
Within arid zones:					
Pastoral tract	6113	(1981)	54209	(1983)	8.86
Rainfed tract	6692	(1981)	23154	(1983)	3.46
Irrigated tract	6295	(1981)	10572	(1983)	1.68

Growth rate of livestock and human population was highest within the tracts of arid zone of Rajasthan as compared to the arid zone of Rajasthan and Rajasthan state as a whole. Extent of increase in both the parameters is given in Table 18.

Table – 18:Comparative mean annual growth rate of livestock and human population.

Area	Mean annual growth rate Livestock %	Population Period	Human %	Population Period
Rajasthan	1.94	1956 - 83	2.85	(1901-81)
Rajasthan arid zone within arid zone.	5.02	1956 - 83	3.63	(1901-81)
Pastoral tract	11.97	1961 - 83	4.75	(1901-81)
Rainfed tract	5.49	1961 - 83	2.58	(1901-81)
Irrigated tract	1.06	1956 - 83	3.61	(1901-81)

Of human population, livestock rearing is traditional functional specialisation of different castes and communities of the region. **Raika**is the most predominant traditional livestock rearing community. **Gujjars, Rajputs, Jats, Mali and Seervi** also rear livestock in addition to cultivation. The Gujjars are good at animal husbandry and graze cattle, buffaloes and sheep. The Jats are the best farmers and cattle breeders. Various other traditonally non-livestock rearing communities like Brahmins, Meghwals, Suthars, Daroga, and others had also taken up livestock rearing as their subsidiary occupation; social customs urging accumulation of wealth in the form of livestock viz. quantity rather than quality and substituting risks of crop failures with large number of animals.

Overstocking of animals leading to overgrazing are often the consequence of a demographic increase higher than the basic productive capacities of the habitat. Thus, for the livestock raisers, the region demands both the maintenance of the habitat's productivity and a population density that does not lead automatically to the multiplication of livestock. **Overstocking in the area leads to nomadic pastoralism which is inherently self-destructive, since systems of management are based on the short term objective of keeping as many animals as possible without**

regard to the long term conservation of land resources. The trend depicts steadily increasing stock numbers on progressively deteriorating land. Thus not only the number of head of livestock but also that of human beings assumes significance.

Analysis of data on animal-human relationship and people's responses have revealed the following causes of increase in livestock:–

- Increased human population have resulted in greater need for livestock as a means of eking out a living.
- Health care programmes for animals have widely and effectively been introduced thereby reducing livestock mortality.
- Periods of favourable weather have enabled herds to grow and multiply.
- Because the only way of saving for many pastoralists is through herd - their bank account - they tend to increase herd size.
- Emergency feeding programme during drought have contributed to the build up of animal number or at least prevented a decrease.
- Pastoralists make consistent efforts in building animal populations beyond the capacity of natural resources.[11]

Livestock population:trend and growth

According to livestock census of Rajasthan, livestock population in the ecological regions of arid zone of Rajasthan had increased considerably during 1951-'83 (Table 19). Increase registered from 32.48 million in 1956 to 49.48 million in 1983 giving a net increase of 52.34% in state of Rajasthan. Whereas, in arid zone of Rajasthan livestock had increased from 9.90 million in 1951 to 223.32 million in 1983 with a net increase of 135.56%. Amongst various ecological regions, pastoral tract revealed an alarming situation for the planners as it had the highest livestock growth of 263.26% during 1961-'83. In the rainfed tract livestock population had increased by 121% during the period of 1961- 83. While in the irrigated tract livestock had increased by about 28% during the period of 1956-83.

Table – 19 : Growth of livestock population in Rajasthan, Arid Zone of Rajasthan and different ecological regions of the Arid Zone of Rajasthan.

Year	Rajasthan		Arid Zone		Ecological Regions of Arid Zone of Rajasthan					
					Pastoral tract Variation		Rainfed tract Variation		Irrigated tract Variation	
	No. Mill-ion	Vari-ation (%)	No. Mill-ion	Vari-ation (%)	No.	(%)	No.	(%)	No.	(%)
1951	-	-	9.0	-	-	-	-	-	-	-
1952	32.48	-	13.40	+35.37	-	-	-	-	8,225	-
1961	33.51	+ 3.16	13.72	+ 2.36	14,923	-	10,482	-	-	-
1966	37.48	+11.83	16.21	+18.15	31,677	+112.14	11.229	+ 7.13	10,532	+28.05
1972	38.88	+ 3.73	16.28	+ 0.48	33,438	+ 5.62	13,971	+24.41	14,517	+37.83
1977	41.36	+ 6.38	19.02	+16.81	39,989	+ 19.59	15,191	+ 8.73	11,369	-21.68
1983	49.48	19.63	23.32	+22.60	54,209	+ 35,56	23,154	+52.42	10,572	- 7.01
Overall Variation		+52.34 (1956-83)		+135.56 (1951-83)		+263.26 (1961-83)		+120.89 (1961-83)		+28.53 (1951-83)

Source: Livestock Census Records, Rajasthan Revenue Board, Ajmer.

Based on rainfall data and villagers' perception of the nature of year, the year like 1951, 52, 54, 55, 57, 59, 1960, 62-63, 68-69, 1971, 72, 74, 1975-77, 1980-83 and 1984-86 were found to be severe droughts and famines (250 mm mean annual rainfall) occuring during various livestock census periods reducing livestock population due to mortality and less production. Despite such recurring drought features of the arid zone of Rajasthan, the livestock had considerably increased by 35% during 1951-56; 2.36% in 1956-61; 18.15% in 1961-66 and 22.6% in 1977-83. The increase also seems to be associated with the occurrence of even one good year in a census period. The years like 1953, 1958, 1961, 1964, 1967, 1970 and 1983 were found to be actual good years accelerating growth of livestock compensating the drought impacts. Whereas, cumulative effect of droughts and famines during 1956 - 61, 1966 - 72 and onwards had hampered the growth, of livestock. Pastoral and rainfed tracts as compared to irrigated one had highest increase of 112% and 52% during 1961-66 and 1977-83 respectively. On the contrary livestock had decreased by 7% and 21% in the irrigated tract during the period of 1972-77 and 1977-83 respectively.

According to recent livestock census (1977-'83), livestock population had on an overall increase by about one-fifths in the state of **Rajasthan** and more than that in its arid zone. Among various types of livestock, sheep followed by goats, cattle, buffaloes and camels were the most predominant types of livestock in the area. Extent and growth of different types of livestock population differed in various regions surveyed (Table 20).

Table – 20 : Growth of Different Types of Livestocks in Rajasthan, Arid Zone of Rajasthan and different Ecological Areas of Arid Zone of Rajasthan during the Period of 1977-'83

Area & Year	Type of livestock					
	Cattle	Buffaloes	Sheep	Goat	Camels	Others
Rajasthan						
1977	12.90	5.07	0.94	12.31	0.75	0.26
1983	13.47	6.04	13.39	15.41	0.75	0.44
Variation (%)	+ 4.42	+19.13	+34.71	+25.18	+ 0.0	+69.23

Arid Zone of Rajasthan						
1977	4.03	1.38	6.68	6.16	0.63	0.13
1983	4.56	1.76	8.76	7.45	0.64	0.16
Variation (%)	+13.15	+27.54	+31.14	+20.94	+ 1.59	+23.10
Ecological tracts pastoral						
1977	3980	-	19697	14310	1473	529
1983	7261	20	32348	12516	1287	777
Variation (%)	+ 82.4	+100.00	+64.2	-12.5	-12.6	+46.9
Rainfed						
1977	1804	545	6107	6070	609	56
1983	2995	994	9534	8837	790	4
Variation (%)	+21.90	+82.40	+56.10	+45.60	+29.70	-89.30
Irrigated						
1977	3895	1012	3831	2332	18	281
1983	3065	1196	3710	2496	41	64
Variation (%)	-21.30	-18.20	- 3.20	+ 7.10	+127.80	-77.20

Note: Livestock population in Rajasthan and Arid Zone is in millions.

Data revealed that sheep and goats as compared to other types of livestock had increased alarmingly during the period. In Rajasthan and its arid zone, sheep population had increased by 31-35%, Goats 21-25%, Buffaloes 19-28%; Cattle 4-13%, Goats 21-25%, Buffaloes 19-28%; Cattle 4-13% and camels 0.1.6% during 1977-83. Tractwise growth of different types of livestock population revealed that in the pastoral tract cattle had increased to the maximum (82%) followed by sheep (63%) during the period. In the rainfed tract there was a maximum increase in sheep (56%) followed by goats (46%), camels (30%) and cattle (22%) and goats (7%) while other types of livestock had decreased. Buffaloes which were almost non-existant in the pastoral tract during 1977 had been introduced afterwards and had increased by 82% in the rainfed tract.

Inter-tract variations concluded that amongst tracts, highest growth rate of predominant livestock viz. sheep, goats and cattle took place in the pastoral and rainfed tracts during 1977-'83. It is natural to expect a positive degree of association between the population increase and an increase in the intensity of depletion of natural grazing resources in the tracts. The constant interaction of the population pressure with a given phyto-mass leads to the vulnerability of the eco-system and cause hardships to the pastoral nomads.

Composition of livestock

Livestock composition reveals the nature and extent of different type of livestock's proportion to total livestock. Livestock composition and its change during 1977 to 1983 in arid zone and within ecological regions of arid zone of Rajasthan is give in Table 21.

Data revealed that of the total livestock of arid zone of Rajasthan (1983), sheep population constituted maximum (37.6%) followed by goats (32%), cattle (19.5%), buffaloes (7.5%), camels (2.7%) and others (0.7%). There was no significant increase or decrease in its composition during the period of 1977-'83. But the composition differed in different ecological regions of arid zone of Rajasthan. Type of land, nature and extent of population inhabiting the region and traditional caste occupational skill of livestock rearing were the main factors influencing number and type of livestock and its composition in a region.

In a pastoral tract composition of livestock population revealed predominance of sheep and goats together constituting more than fourfifths of total livestock during 1977 and 1983. Cattle constituted about one tenths; camel and others less than four per cent while buffaloss were negligible. A significant change had been in the composition of cattle, sheep and goats. Cattle and sheep had increased from 9.9% and 49.3% in 1977 to 13.5% and 59.7% respectively in 1983. While goats and camels decreased from 35.8% amd 3.7% in 1977 to 23.1% and 2.4% respectively in 1983. There was almost no change in buffaloes and other category of livestock in the pastoral tract.

Rainfed tract had also predominance of sheep and goats together constituting 80% of total livestock during 1977 and 1983. In the irrigated tract also, sheep and goats together were predominant comprising of more than half of total livestock.

Comparison of livestock composition (1983) in various tracts revealed that cattle constituted highest (29%) in the irrigated tract,

Table – 21 : Percentage composition of livestock in Arid Zone of Rajasthan and its different Ecological Regions

Livestock	Arid zone of Rajasthan		Pastoral tract		Rainfed tract		Irrigated tract	
	1977	1983	1977	1983	1977	1983	1977	1983
Cattle	21.2	19.5	9.9	13.4	11.9	12.9	34.3	29.0
Buffaloes	7.3	7.5	neg	0.1	3.6	4.3	8.9	11.3
Sheep	35.1	37.6	49.3	59.7	40.2	41.2	33.7	35.1
Goat	32.4	32.0	35.8	23.1	39.9	38.2	20.5	23.6
Camel	3.3	2.7	3.7	2.4	4.0	3.3	0.2	0.4
Other	0.7	0.7	1.3	1.3	0.4	0.1	2.4	0.6
Total	100.0	100.0	100.0	100.0	100.0	100.0	100.0	100.0

Sheep and goats together were maximum (83%) in the pastoral tract and minimum (55%) in the irrigated tract. Whereas camels constituted highest percentage (4%) in the rainfed and pastoral as compared to the irrigated one.

It is thus concluded that higher the aridity of the tract having more fallow and duny lands for grazing, higher the number of sheep and goats conducive to more desertic conditions of the area. On the other hand, higher the irrigation facility and lesser aridity with more scopes for cultivation allowing lesser grazing lands, higher the number of cattle and buffaloes in the area and lesser sheep and goats.[12]

Livestock pressure

Increase in the livestock population has led to the overstocking of the permanent pastures and other grazing lands in the area. The **Raikas** and **Sindhi** Muslims,the traditional sheep and goat raisers, followed by **Rajputs** and **Jats** who had taken up sheep and goat rearing as a profitable occupation supported the fact of gradual shrinkage of grazing lands for the animals. This has been revealed through high density or pressure of livestock in terms of adult cattle unit per ha. of any type of land-use category (Table 22).

Table – 22: Density of Adult Livestock Units/100 ha of Land Use Category in Arid Zone of Rajasthan and Ecological Regions.

Regionwise type of land	Density of livestock 100 ha of 1977	adult units/ land 1983	Increase in livestock density % (1977-'83)
I. **Arid Zone of Rajasthan**			
. Total area	35	43	22.86
. Permanent and pastures & other grazing lands	884	1017	15.05
. Total grazing lands available	79	95	20.25
. Net area sown	75	85	13.33
II. **Pastoral tract**			
. Total area	30	40	33.33

. Permanent pastures and other grazing lands	552	708	35.6
. Total grazing lands available	37	50	35.14
. Net area sown	152	206	35.53
III. Rainfed Tract			
. Total area	40	61	52.50
. Permanent pastures and other grazing lands	894	1362	52.35
. Total grazing lands available	125	191	52.80
. Net area sown	58	89	53.45
IV. Irrigated tract			
. Total area	38	36	-5.26
. Permanent pastures and other grazing lands	613	570	-7.01
. Total grazing lands available	77	72	-6.49
. Net area sown	76	70	-7.89

Data revealed that in arid zone of Rajasthan, density of adult livestock units per 100 ha of per area sown and total geographical area was found to be 1017, 95, 85 and 43 respectively during the year 1983. The livestock pressure in all the cases had increased from minimum 13% to maximum 23% during the period of 1977-83. Density of the livestock was quite high as compared to an optimum desirable pressure of 20 adult cattle units per 100 ha of permanent pastures and other grazing lands under these conditions.

Livestock ownership

Livestock-raising households make a living from their animals by maintaining sufficient number of animals. Herd sizes are determined by human manipulation under low technology conditions of subsistence pastoralism, due to uncontrolled environmental stresses of disasters. The keeping of large herds is closely linked to the need to protect the household against the effects of drought or epidemicsas well as to food requirements during a particular dry period. A sufficient number of animals must survive a disaster in order that the household can exist while the herd is being rebuilt.

Summing Up

The desertic conditions in North-western region are believed to have developed as a result of meterological, geological and hydrological change over the centuries. But the process has been accentuated by the activities of man inhabiting these areas. Due to unsuitability of the land for crop farming and the latter being a gamble on the desert land, its inhabitants had to resort to livestock farming as the main source of subsistence. In short livestock farming has traditionally been one of the most viable elements of the agro-economic system of the arid zone of Rajasthan.

The nomadic pastoralists inhabiting the Rajasthan desert have been depending on livestock breeding for generations and have contributed significantly to the economy of the region by the providing wool, mutton, hides and skins, etc. They inhabited and utilized the areas which were relatively more arid and less suitable for cultivation of crops, and hence they rightly utilized these lands as pasturage for their livestock.

The arid zone society in the past has been frequently exposed to high mortality rate. Thus society not only permitted but encouraged high fertility rates in human population. Thus, arid Rajasthan has higher growth rate than Rajasthan as a whole, and Rajasthan has a higher rate than the whole of India. Spread over an area of 208 sq.kms the Rajasthan arid zone has a population of 13.40 millions (1981). The region has an average density of 64 persons per sq.km and is one of the most thickly populated deserts of the world. The growth rate of population (1901 - 1981) in the arid zone of Rajasthan (excluding Ganganagar district where the rise has been mainly due to immigration of population) was 249% as comparead to the Rajasthan State (231%) and of the country as a whole (187%) . Similarly, within the arid zone of Rajasthan the percentage increase in the population during the period 1901 - 1981 has been 279%, 260%, and 219% in the regions receiving annual rainfall of less than 12", between 12" - 16" and above 16" respectively.

The increasing human population is a serious stress, particularly on the vegetal resources of the desert. The trees and shrubs and even their roots are indiscriminately cut by the rural population for fuel, top, feed, fencing and the construction of thatched hutments. It has been estimated that the requirements of the people in the desert in respect of the woody biomass has increased from 1.85 million tonnes in 1951 to 3.33 million tonnes in 1971. Moreover, the desert people have developed peculiar food habits. All the available air-dried seeds and pods of the trees are used as delicacies. The seeds of **Acacia senegal (Kumat),** the fruits of **Capparis decidua (Kair)** and the pods of **Prosopis cineraria (Sangri)** are harvested. Almost all the fruits of **Zizyphus nummularia (ber, Jhadberi)** growing in accessible parts of the desert are harvested for human consumption. The seeds of grasses, e.g. **Panicum turqidum, P. antidotale, Cenchrus biflorus and Echinochlo colonum,** are mixed with millet for making chapatis (unleavened cakes) especially during drought years. The grass seeds are supposed to add to the nutritive value of the food. The intensity with which seed collection is made for direct human consumption throughout the desert region seriously affects the natural process of regeneration of the desirable plant species in the inhospitable terrain.

In spite of the low productivity of the arid land, Rajasthan sustains a fairly high population of livestock. If we examine livestock census data pertaining to the desert districts of Rajasthan from the census year 1956 to the census year 1983 - a period covering 27 years. - certain interesting facts emerge. During this period, cattle registered the lowest (23%) growth rate, sheep (81%) and goat (86%) populations had very high growth rates while buffaloes have registered a strikingly high growth rate of 125 per cent (which is possibly more of an indication of increased availability of water in the region through canals and dug wells in recent times than anything else). The region, thus, had 73% more livestock to feed in 1983 than in 1956. This staggering increase in animal numbers is also reflected in the quantum jump in the human : livestock ratio of 100 : 117 a decade back to that of 100: 173 within the desert region today, there being nearly 13.4 million human beings in the 11 desert districts of Rajasthan according to the 1981 census report. Incidentally, while the decennial - 1971 (10.2m) - 1981 (13.4m) - increase in human population in the arid zone of Rajasthan has been almost 31.3 per cent, the livestock population during the 11-year period 1972 (16.3m) - 1983 (23.2m) increased by more than 42 per cent.

Under the influence of man when the exploitation of natural resources exceeds replacement by nature, the ecology moves towards negative side of the homeostatic plateau. Increased livestock population has got a direct correlation with the high growth rate of human population and its demand. The growth of population has affected the degree of intensity of land use by putting more sub-marginal lands under agriculture or intensive use of lands already under cultivation and intensive grazing of fastly shrinking pasture land. During the last three decades the net area sown has increased tremendously but the area under less intensive use has considerably decreased as revealed by the decline in fallow lands, wasteland and uncultivable barren wastelands. The overall grazing land has decreased significantly while the population of grazing animals has increased substantially during this period. This aspect is discussed in more detail in the next chapter.

A positive degreee of association persists between the livestock population increase and in the intensity of depletion of grazing lands. Fast increase in livestock population inspite of gradual shrinkage in the extent of grazing lands has resulted in over-exploitation of grazing lands and also to partial starvation of livestock. Consequences of too many livestock using grazing grounds are partial starving of livestock due to shortage of grasses, land getting spoiled and becoming weaker, and soil erosion due to trampling of livestock. As an adjustment mechanism, more and more pastoralist are now resorting to long distances seasonal migration, and not returning to the area along with their flocks and instead moving permanently in search of fodder in harvested fields, rangelands and forests.

REFERENCES

1. Dickson, B.T. 1957. Guide Book to Research Data for Arid Zone Development, UNESCO PARIS.
2. Ibid.
3. Malhotra, S.P and J.C. Kalla. 1990 Social and Economic Constraints in Optimal Land Use under Arid Conditions.
4. Ibid.
5. Salzman, P.C. 1986. Shrinking Pasture For Rajasthani Pastoralists. In Nomadic Peoples-Commission On Nomadic Peoples. IUAES, No. 20.
6. Dhir, R.P. 1988. Flux in the Indian Arid Zone. In Desert Ecology (ed.) by Ishwar Prakash Scientific Publishers Jodhpur.

7. ——1982. The Human Factor In Ecological History. In Desertification and Development : Dryland Ecology in Social Perspective (ed.) by B.Spooner and H.S. Mann. Academic Press, London.

8. Op.cit. Malhotra, S.P. and J.C. Kalla.

9. Jain, M.M. 1986. Growth Pattern of Dairy Sub-sector in Rajasthan. **Himalaya Publishing House.** Bombay.

10. Bharara, L.P. 1988 Animal Human Relationship and Desertification in Arid Zone. In Desertification : Monitoring & Control (ed.) by A.K. Tiwari. Scientific Publishers. Jodhpur.

11. Ibid.

12. Ibid.

4

Declining Grazing Resources and Pastoral Nomadism

Grazing Resources of India

Grazing based animal husbandry plays an important role in the rural economy of India. About 406 million livestock population in India mainly thrives on the grazing resources. The grazing activity is mainly dependent on the availability of the grazing resources from pastures and other grazing lands viz., forests, miscellaneous tree crops and grooves, cultivable wastelands and fallow lands. The total area available for grazing accounts for about 40 per cent of the geographical area of India[1] (Fig. 8). A variety of grazing systems are practised in different climatic zones where pastoralism is the way of life.

The 67.33 million ha of **forests** cover 22.1% of India's geographical area and are important as a source of forage and grazing (Fig. 9). Simiarly, the 12 m ha **pastures** account for 3.94% of the geographical area of the country and form the main grazing resource. In the arid and semi- arid region of north-western India, which mainly includes the states of Rajasthan and Gujarat, there is a vast area available for grazing viz. over 40 per cent in Rajasthan of which **pastures** and **wastelands** constitute about 5.4 and 16.4 per cent respectively. But in extremely arid districts nearly 80 percent of the area is available for grazing whereas in other parts it is about 50 per cent. The sourthern part of Rajasthan, which is mainly hilly, has about 50 per cent grazing area.

In Gujarat, about 30 per cent area is used for grazing of which 3.5 and 10.56 per cent are **pastures** and **cultivable wastelands.**

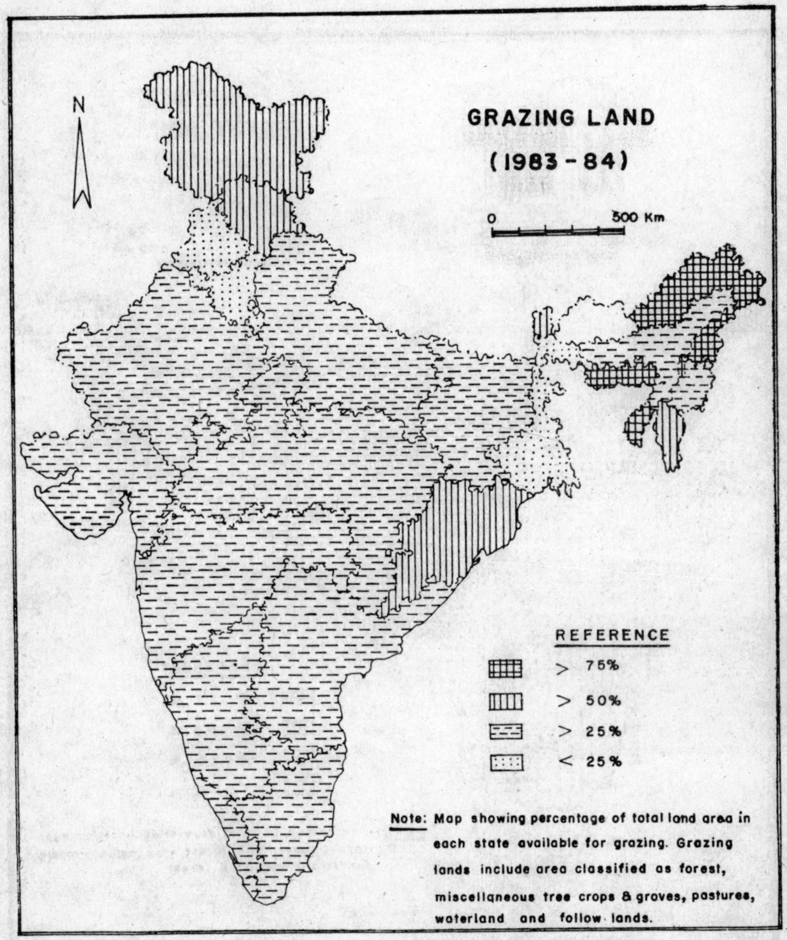

Fig. 8

Source : IGFRI, Jhansi.

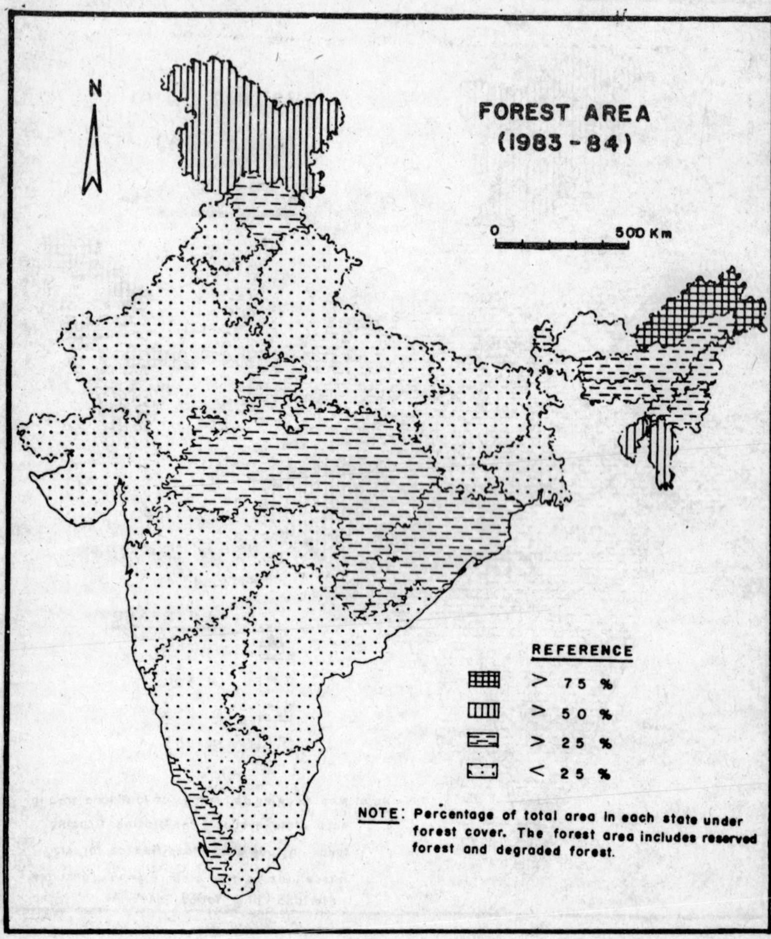

Fig. 9
Source : IGFRI, Jhansi.

Gujarat's living desert **Banni** a long tract of land in **Kuchch,** is one of the largest grasslands in Asia.

The total area under **miscellaneous tree crops and grooves** is about 3.46 m ha. which constitutes 1.14 per cent of the toal geographical area of India. All of these are situated in the north-eastern part of the country which is a mountaineous region and receives heavy rainfall favouring the growth of forests and miscellaneous tree crops and grooves. However, grazing is not much popular here. Other states have negligible areas of this category.

The **cultivable wastelands** are presently used for grazing. Of the toal reporting area of the country, 5.1 per cent land is under cultivable wastelands. The States of Meghalaya (20.19%), Rajasthan (16.77%), and Gujarat (10.56%) have relatively larage proportion of cultivable wastelands, whereas, other States have around 5%.

The combined area under **permanent pastures** and other **grazing lands** covers about 10 per cent of the total geographical area of India. The significantly high percentage has been observed in Himachal Pradesh (41.75%) followed by States of Meghalaya (20.40%), Nagaland (23.57%), Rajasthan (22.40%), Gujarat (15.07%) and Sikkim (13.72%).

Fallow lands are widely used for grazing or hay and cover about 22.9 m ha of land constituting 7.5 per cent of the total land area of India. These are more prominent in the States of Nagaland (32.28%), Bihar (18.26%), Tamil Nadu (16.14%), Meghalaya (13.87%), Andhra Pradesh (11.72%) and Rajasthan (11.10%). The other States have below 10 per cent area under this category . The cultivated area is left fallow mainly due to lack of rainfall as in Tamil Nadu, Andhra Pradesh and Rajasthan or heavy rainfall as in Meghalaya, Nagaland and Bihar. But the use of fallow lands is mostly restricted to their owners. The **Community** or **Panchayat grazing lands** are showing a deceasing trend due to various reasons. A large part of it now has been transferred to landless persons which has resulted in the acute scarcity of village pasture lands.[2]

Grazing Resources of Semi-arid and Arid Regions

Grazing based animal husbandry is the predominant occupation and the major source of livelihood of the people in the arid regions. In the semi-arid regions, however, dry farming is the major occupation and livestock rearing has a subsidiary role to play in the agricultural economy. This is reflected in the land coverage of **rangelands** of grazing lands in the two regions. In the semi-arid zone, the rangelands occupy 15 to 20% land, and are of small sizes located on marginal or even degraded lands earmarked as community grazing lands. In the arid regions, the rangelands occupy on an average 45% land and in extreme arid tracts like Jaisalmer district of the Rajasthan State, 95% of the total district area (41674.3 sq.km) is used as **rangelands** or **grazing** lands. The degraded lands viz. **ravines** and areas of problem soils viz. **saline depressions** and **flats** provide a considerable amount of grazing in the semi-arid zone. The saline land, which is nearly 4% of the total land area and **sandy land forms** viz. **dunes and hummocky** undulations provide meagre grazing in the arid zones[3].

Both semiarid and arid grazing lands bear the brunt of past misuse and present neglect. The grazing pressure on semi-arid rangelands is estimated[4] at 3.2 ACU/ha whereas a rangelands (eg **Sehima-Heteropogon**) of good range condition has the carrying capacity of 1 ACU/ha. The situation in arid rangelands is rather different. In the accessible tracts the rangelands are overgrazed and so, are generally of 'poor' range condition. As against carrying capacity of 0.2 to 0.5 ACU/ha[5] the grazing pressure ranges 5 from 1 to 4 ACU/ha. In the areas which have a large inaccessible tract and drinking water problem viz. Jaisalmer district of the State of Rajasthan, there is a surplus dry forage of 1.46 mt from the 39480 sq.km of the grass cover and the district can support twice the present strength of the livestock, and if improved and managed well, can support four times of the present livestock[6].

Grazing resources of semiarid regions

Of the available grazing area in the semiarid regions permanent pastures occupy slightly over 5% area but comparatively much larger grazing area is available in forests (14.09%) and wastelands (8.65%). Total 31.65% area in the semiarid zone is available for grazing (Table 23). In some states in the semiarid zone the grazing intensity (number of animals per hecatare) is very high viz., 1.68 in Punjab. 1.6 in Haryana and very low viz. 0.23 in Madhya Pradesh and 0.38 in Maharashtra. By and large, if we exclude the area under forests and miscellaneous tree crops and groves, the grazing resources in other areas are not adequate as these are in various stages of degradation[7].

Table 23 : Grazing Resources in different states of the Semiarid regions of India (Thousand heactares)

State	Total geographical area	Forests	Pastures	Mis.tree crops & groves	Waste land	Fallow land	Total grazing resources
Punjab	3513	163	–	–	11	25	3712
Haryana	3094	136	59	1	23	117	3430
Uttar Pradesh	7531	326	29	115	266	402	8669
Rajasthan	16170	1954	1645	16	1083	692	21560
Gujarat	10938	985	643	–	222	642	13430
Madhya Pradesh	12364	2988	754	5	430	309	16850
Maharashtra	22503	3900	1002	86	404	1223	29118
Karnataka	14434	1667	1244	166	341	1234	19087
Andhra Pradesh	19964	3330	711	421	603	3961	28990
Tamil Nadu	11766	1789	119	190	297	1978	16139
Total	122277	17238	6207	1000	3680	10583	160985
Percent of total geographical area		4.09	5.07	0.81	3.00	8.65	31.65

Degraded forests

Forests, whether of climax status or at any stage in primary or secondary sere are liable to be degraded to various degrees through biotic influences, notably excessive grazing, lopping for fodder, green manure or fuel and irregulated fellings for timber, poles and fuel. Sometimes one or more trees are left out in the degraded forests which are extensively used as grazing grounds.

Grass cover

The grass cover of the semiarid zone correspond broadly to the **Sehima Dichanthium** type but in the north- west **Dichanthium - Cenchrus - Lasiurus** type also occurs in same parts[9].

Sehima-Dichanthium type

This grass cover is spread over throughout the peninsular India, including the Central Indian Plateau, the Chhotanagpur Plateau and the Aravalli Ranges, covering 12 states namely Gujarat, Maharashtra, Madhya Pradesh, Orissa, Andhra Pradesh, Karnataka, Tamil Nadu and Kerala as well as south-west Bengal, southern Bihar and the southern hilly portions of Uttar Pradesh and Rajasthan. The total area under this grass cover is about 1,740,000 sq.km.

Dichanthium - Cenchrus - Lasiurus type

This type is associated with subtropical arid and semiarid regions comprising the northern portion of Gujarat, whole of Rajasthan, excluding the Aravallis, western Uttar-Pradesh, Delhi and Punjab with a potential coverage of over 436 sq. km.

Highest development of the cover is **Dichanthium** type on heavier soils, Cenchrus type on loamy to sandy loam soils and Lasiurus type on sandy soils.

Fodders and feeds

The semiarid zones have, by and large, dry farming system of crop production where major consideration is for grain crops. Sole cropping of fodder crops viz., sorghum and cowpea is meagre. The practice at present is to feed the livestock with crop residues viz., straws and stovers from the grain crops. There is a pretty long lean period 6 to 8 months and fodder scarcity, specially during droughts, is acute.

Grazing resources of arid regions

Over 60% arid area lies in western Rajasthan and over 20% in the western part of Gujarat state. In these rangelands, there are few scattered thorny trees with a spinkling of shrubs, some of which have high forage value. Rangelands include not only grasslands but also forest grazing areas, culturable and non-culturable lands current and old fallows. The area under grazingland has declined by 23.78 per cent from 1951 to 1971-72 and is estimated to have further declined during the last 16 years, building a greater pressure on grazing resources[9]. The rangelands of the arid zones have the following grass cover type[10].

1. **Senima nervosum** : type (on hills and piedmonts)
2. **Dilchanthium annualatum type** (on old alluvium),
3. **Cenchrus type** (on well drained sandy alluvial soils),
4. **Lasirus Sindicus** type (on loose sandy soil),
5. **Desmonstachya bipinnata** type **(on young alluvium)**, and
6. **Sporobolus marginatus-Dichanthiu annulatum** type (on low lying heavy saline soils).

Condition of Grazing lands

In the extensive survey of range resources in different parts of arid zone, condition classification of grazing land as proposed by USDA was adopted after little modification by **Shankar** and **Kumar** in the survey of the Luni basin, Jaisalmer and Jalore. The emerging picture is that over 70 per cent of the grazing lands have poor to very poor condition class. Of the remaining nearly 13 per cent belong to the 'good' class, 14 per cent to the 'fair' class and 2 - 3 per cent could be assigned to 'excellent' status (Fig. 10). This indicates the severity of biotic degradation by increasing livestock[11].

Availability of Grazing Resources

Assessment of grazing resource availability is to be viewed in the light of the increasing livestock population and declining range productivity. The pressure of increasing livestock as expressed in adult cattle units (ACU) is strikingly on an increase from 1961 to 1966, 1972, 1977 and 1981 in all districts of western Rajasthan

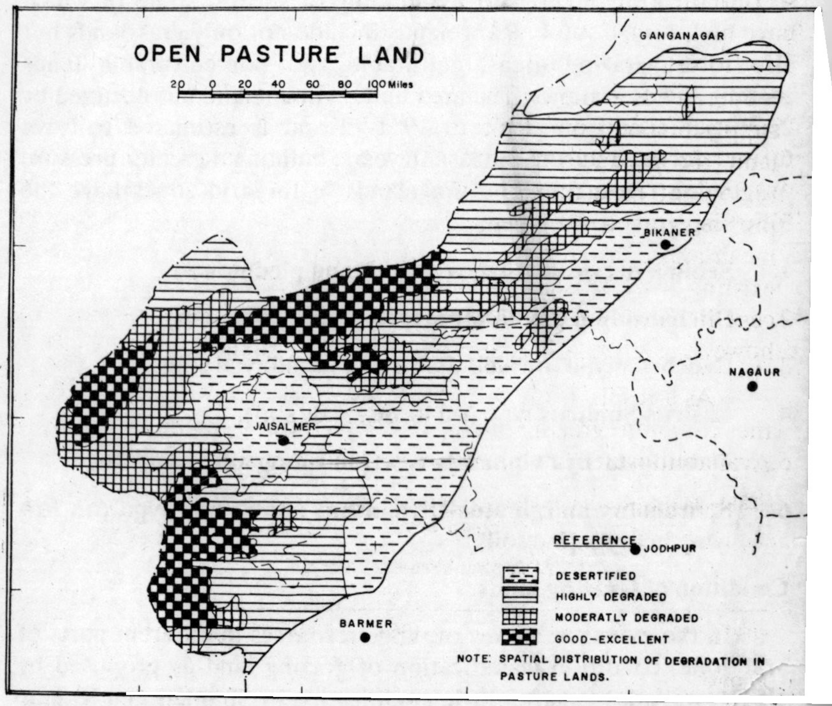

Fig. 10

Source : R.P. Dhir, 1990, Land Degradation in the Bird Zone, CAZRI, Jodhpur.

(Table 24). The increase in livestock also results in decline in effective area of grazing land available for each livestock (Fig. 11). **Shankarnarayan**[12] estimated that from 1972 to 1977 in 12 districts of western Rajasthan, grazing land per livestock has declined (Table 25) to the tune of 7 to 97 per cent.

The most essential things needed for livestock production are fodder, feeds, water etc. Unfortunately these are in alarmingly short supply in the arid regions of Western Rajasthan. Availability of land, the produces of feeds and fodder, and its utilization in arid regions of Rajasthan is given in Table 26. It is obvious that the pressure of cultivation and livestock is higher into zone B where the mean annual rainfall is above 300mm. The shortage of forage for existing livestock population amounts to 42.0, 35.0 and 35.1 per cent in Zone A, B and total arid zone respectively. Situation is, however, alarming during years of scanty rainfall[13].

As a result of the pressure of livestock and human population, the common grazing lands have decreased (Table 27 & 28). Availability of 8.7m ha of grazing lands is erroneous in the sense it

Table 24 :Livestock Population expressed in Million Adult Cattle Units (ACUs) in north-western Rajasthan

(After Shankarnarayan & Kalla, 1985)

District	1961	1966	1972	1977	1981
Barmer	8.58	10.68	8.04	7.98	12.98
Bikaner	5.23	6.48	5.21	5.28	11.93
Churu	3.39	3.90	4.98	6.32	7.14
Ganganagar	6.32	6.87	8.34	9.48	11.94
Jaisalmer	3.00	3.64	1.87	2.22	4.91
Jalore	4.78	5.63	4.98	5.44	5.95
Jhunjhunu	3.23	3.15	3.92	4.45	4.77
Jodhpur	4.78	5.74	6.20	8.47	8.73
Nagaur	4.78	5.74	6.20	8.47	8.73
Pali	6.52	7.42	7.44	8.29	7.89
Sikar	4.16	4.61	5.79	5.78	6.66
Total	54.72	64.38	64.61	76.33	86.56

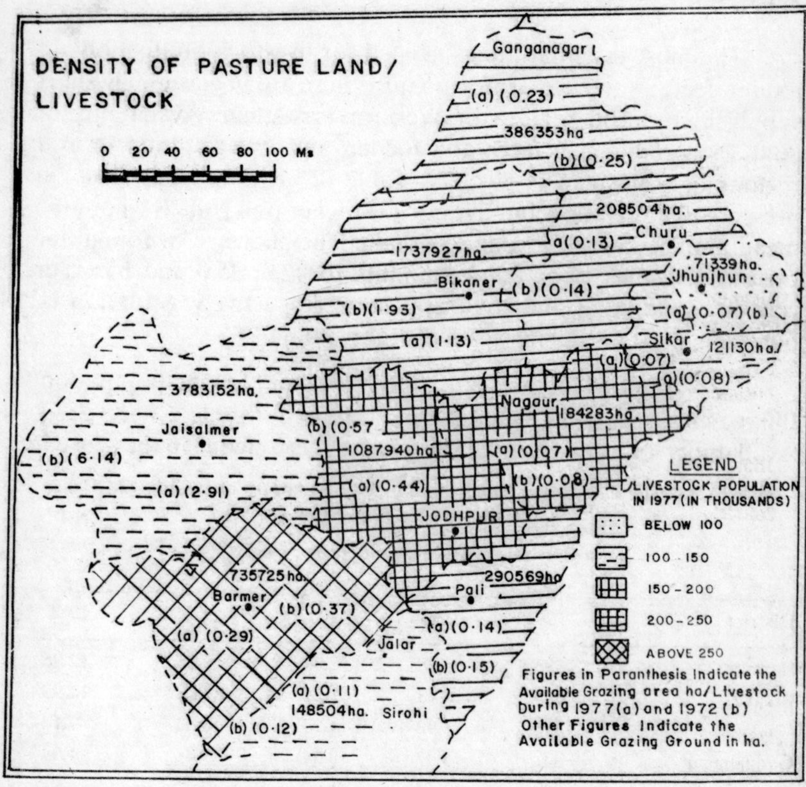

Fig. 11

Source : T.S. Chouhan, 1988, Livestock Development in Drylands of Rajasthan, in ed.vol. Current Practices in Dryland Resources & Technology, Diyajyoti Prakashan, Jodhpur.

comprises permanent pasture lands, wastelands and marginal lands. In the pasture grounds of 8.8m ha. 7.0 m ha of wastelands and 0.89 m ha marginal lands are also included. Actually only 0.91m ha permanent pasture lands are available in this region which is only 4.3% of the total area for cultivation. Nonetheless this suggests that 7.9m ha of wastelands and marginal lands are available for 14 development of pasture lands[14].(Fig. 12)

Table 25: Extent and availability of grazing and per unit of livestock in 12 districts of western Rajasthan (After Shankarnarayan, 1985)

District	Land area (ha)	Grazing lands (% of the land area)	Grazing land livestock (ha) 1972	1977	Decline %
Bikaner	2885072	60.2	1.93	1.13	41.45
Barmer	2817294	26.1	0.37	0.29	21.62
Churu	1685114	12.4	0.14	0.13	7.14
Jodhpur	2217800	49.1	0.57	0.44	22.80
Jaisalmer			6.14	2.91	52.60
Gangangar	2041446	19.0	0.25	0.23	8.00
Sikar	774925	15.6	0.98	0.08	91.83
Jhunjhunu	542730	12.3	0.07	0.07	0
Nagaur			0.08	0.07	12.5
Jalore	1056357	14.1	0.12	0.11	8.33
Pali	1229762	23.6	6.15	0.14	97.72

Table 26 : Land and livestock pressure in arid districts of Rajasthan

Agaro-climatic zone	Total area 000'ha	Area 000'ha		Total live stock ACU (Milli ons)	Land available in ha/ ACU			Forage shortage per yr. per cent
		Under cultivation	Under grazing		Total	Cultivable	Grazing	
Zone A	11,498	3610 (30.4)	5785 (50.4)	2.043	5.63	1.76	1.83	42.0
Zone B	9,361	57.41 (61.3)	1777 (29.7)	4.690	1.996	1.22	0.59	35.0
Total	20,859	93.51 (44.8)	8562 (41.1)	6.733	3.09	1.38	1.27	35.1

Zone 'A' indicates areas with mean annual rainfall below 300 mm

Figures in parenthesis indicate percentage

Zone 'B' indicates areas with mean annual rainfall above 300 m

ACU = Adult Cattle Units

Table 27: Extent of grazing lands in western Rajasthan

		1951-52	1971-72	1977-78
1.	Area of grazing land (m/ha)	11.3	9.2	8.7
2.	Share(%) of total geographical area	60.5	47.9	45.1
3.	Animal units per 100 ha of common grazingland	39	94.0	105.0

Source: The State of India's Environment 1984-85, New Delhi.

Table 28: Pasture grounds in western Rajasthan

Total area (ha)	Pasture lands Permanent pasture	(in ha) Wastelands	Marginal lands	Total pasture lands
2,12,04,211	9,11,233	70,50,577	8,93,691	88,56,101
% of total area	4.3	33.25	4.21	41.8

The fodder requirement for about 27 million animals in western Rajasthan worked out to about 30 million ton while food grain requirement to feed 17 million human population worked out to 3.40 million ton approx[15]. (Table 29)

Table 29 : Estimated Annual Fodder requirement of Western Rajasthan (As per Livestock Census 1983)

(D.M. Basis)

Sl. No.	Animal Spp.	Population (Lakh)	Fooder reqd./ animal/ day (Kg.)	Fodder reqd./ animal/year (Qtl.)	Annual fodder requirement (Million Ton)
1.	Cattle	45.7	8.0	29.20	13.34
2.	Buffalo	17.6	10.0	36.50	6.42
3.	Goat	74.5	1.3	4.75	3.54
4.	Sheep	87.7	1.0	3.65	3.20
5.	Camel	6.5	12.0	43.80	2.85
6.	Horse + Pony	0.1	8.0	29.20	0.03
7.	Others	1.3	8.0	29.20	0.38
	Total				29.76
				Say	30.0

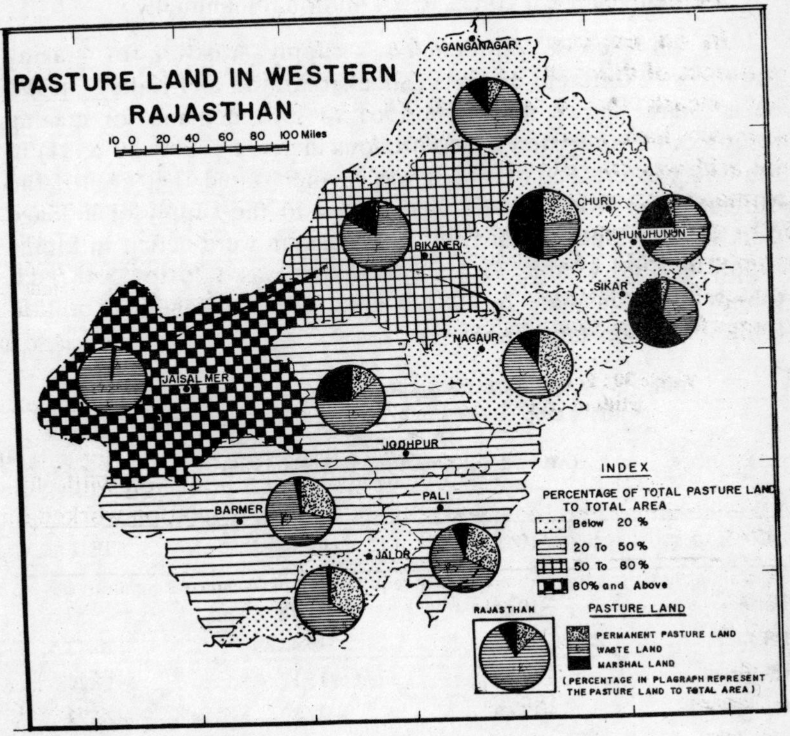

Fig. 12

Source : T.S. Choushan, 1988.

In 1990 fodder requirement is expected to be 36.0 (20% increase)

Food grain required for 170 lakh human population at 2 quintal/head/year comes to 3.4 million ton annually.

In an exercise on demand - supply situation of grazing resources of different districts (Shankarnarayan and Kalla)[16], it has been clearly shown that from 1961 to 1981 demand for grazing resources have registered a continuous increase (Table 30 & 31) in the arid western Rajasthan. It was further stated that even if the estimates for crop residues were added to the supply of herbage from grazing lands, 10 districts of Rajasthan were deficit in forage supply in 1981 (Table 31) . This deficit was 1.26 to 13.48 lakh tonnes for Rajasthan. In 1981, a total deficit of about 6 million tonnes for Rajasthan (Table 32).

Table 30 : Forage demand-supply imbalances (in lakh Tonnes) without crop residues in Arid Zone of north-western Rajasthan
(After Shankarnarayan & Kalla, 1985)

District	1961	1971	1981
Barmer	−19.86	−17.29	−29.97
Bikaner	−9.83	−9.42	−26.43
Churu	−14.18	−15.12	−17.26
Ganganagar	−17.64	−22.80	−28.99
Jaisalmer	−9.21	+1.62	−5.38
Jalore	−8.61	−12.80	−14.06
Jhunjhunu	−6.33	−10.86	−11.54
Jodhpur	−22.29	−19.20	−19.79
Nagaur	−14.06	−21.07	−23.68
Pali	−8.54	−16.91	−15.94
Sikar	−7.24	−13.98	−16.16
Total	−137.89	−157.86	−192.58

Table 31: Demand-supply of grazing resources in Arid Zone of North-western Rajasthan (lakh tonnes) in 1981 (After Shakarnarayan & Kalla, 1985)

State/District	Demand	Supply: Without crop residue	Supply: With crop residue
Barmer	32.46	2.49	24.87
Bikaner	29.83	3.40	16.34
Churu	17.86	0.60	19.97
Ganganagar	29.86	0.87	23.19
Jaisalmer	12.28	6.90	10.96
Jalore	12.87	0.88	9.65
Jhunjhunu	11.82	0.28	6.74
Jodhpur	21.84	2.05	20.57
Nagaur	25.80	2.06	19.81
Pali	19.75	3.80	11.81
Sikar	16.66	0.50	8.04
Total	233.03	23.83	172.00

Table 32: A demand-supply imbalance for forage with crop residues in Arid Zone of north-western Rajasthan (in lakh tonnes) (After Shankarnarayan & Kalla, 1985)

District	1961	1971	1981
Rajasthan			
Barmer	−1.02	−4.03	−7.58
Bikaner	+2.42	+1.63	−13.48
Churu	−7.70	+3.98	+2.10
Ganganagar	−5.00	−0.51	−6.67
Jaisalmer	−1.99	+4.18	−1.31
Jalore	+2.08	−3.57	−5.21
Jhunjhunu	+0.86	−4.23	−5.07
Jodhpur	−12.29	−3.15	−1.26
Nagaur	−6.41	−3.71	−5.99
Pali	+4.85	−8.72	−7.93
Sikar	+2.12	−6.19	−8.61
Total	−22.08	−16.28	−61.06

*1 lakh = 100 thousand

Reasonable fertile soils, highly adapted nature of vegetation and a favourable, though short growing period, all combine to permit a good cover of perennial grasses alongwith a sprinkling of trees and shrubs. In fact the existence of the famous sewan lands (**Lasiurus Sindicus**) in Jaisalmer region bear ample testimony to the potentialilty of this region. However, such excellent cover exists to-day as islands only in most inaccessible parts of th arid zone. A vast majority of the pasture lands are in a state of severe degradation[17]. A distribution and extent of these lands and the estimate of the area is as follows :

Conditon of pasture land	Percentage of the total grassland area
Desertified	24
Highly degraded	44
Moderately degraded	19
Goód to excellent	13

A study conducted by **Kavoori**[18] showed that a considerable number of vegetation types disappeared or are disapperaring with striking frequency from the 4 sampled districts of western Rajasthan. A total number of 106 different types of vegetation comprising 61 types of grasses, 32 types of shrubs and bushes, and 13 varieties of trees were recorded as having disappeared or virtually so. Striking among them was the presence of some of the most valuable and nutritious types of livestock grazing. Thus among the more valued types, **Dhaman** was recorded as having disappeared from 20 of the 45 villages. **Pala** had disappeared from 22, **Ganthiya** from 19, **Laump** and **Bekar** from 16, **Sewan** from 9 villages. In the case of trees, the **Kumbhat** (17), **Desi Bordi** (14), **Kherji** and **Desi Babool** (7) came across as severly endangered. A district wise break-up of details is given in Table 33. As may be seen from the table in the case of grasses as well as in that of shrubs and bushes, it is particularly the more arid districts of Barmer, Jaisalmer, and Jodhpur which show losses of a higher number of vegetation types. Even more significantly, the frequency with which these vegetation types have disappeared is far greater in the arid districts. This pattern is true of all the three vegetation groups. On an average it works out that each village has lost about twelve vegetation types. The frequency table provides a clearer idea of this. We find here that the largest chunk of villages (over 50%), lost anywhere between 15 to 20 types of vegetation, 30% lost between 10 and 15 varieties, and only 15% of the villages can be thought of as having suffered lightly. In the long term therefore there can be little doubt that the arid region has witnessed a deterioration in pasture, in terms of both quality and range.

Table 33: Measures of Decline in Vegetation:

No. of Types of Vegetation Disappeared

	Grass	Shrubs	Trees	Total
Pali	15	13	7	35
Nagaur	16	10	6	32
Jodhpur	26	15	6	47
Barmer	22	19	9	50
Jaisalmer	41	18	7	66

Table 33.1 : Number of Cases Disappeared

	Grass	Shrubs	Trees	Total
Pali	39	27	18	84
Nagaur	33	19	8	60
Jodhpur	56	25	12	93
Barmer	63	60	34	157
Jaisalmer	97	41	13	151
Total	288	172	85	545

Table 33.2 : Frequency Distribution of Number of Cases Disappeared per Village

	0-5	6-10	11-15	16-20	21+	No.of villages
Pali	1	2	2	1	1	7
Nagaur	5	0	0	0	0	10
Jodhpur	1	2	4	1	0	8
Barmer	0	3	2	3	2	10
Jaisalmer	0	2	4	1	3	10
Total	7	14	12	6	6	45

Though arid regions of India are constrained by climatic, edaphic and biotic factors, they support a large diversity of grass and browse species. Distribution of these species is habitat specific; the full optimum expression in terms of cover, vigour and herbage yield is attained at a particular habitat. However, the potential yield is rarely achieved because of increasing biotic pressure. The increasing livestock which graze the biomass too frequently and at shorter intervals allows only very poor growth. This has also resulted in decline in the grazing land area available per livestock.

A positive degree of association persists between the livestock population increase and an increase in the intensity of depletion of grazing lands in the tracts. The constant inter-action of the population pressure with the given phyto-mass leads to vulnerability of the eco-system and thus accentuate the desertification process. **Bharara**[19] found that Livestock pressure differed in various tracts due to different land use parameters sustaining varied livestock pressure. Of all the tracts, rainfed tract had highest livestock pressure (1977-83) of all types of livestock on various land use categories. The livestock pressure was highest (1362 adult livestock units per 100 ha) on permanent pastures and other grazing lands of the rainfed tract whereas pressure on net sown area was highest in the pastoral tract. The reasons of comparatively lower pressure on permanent pastures, on total grazing lands and on total area of a pastoral tract, were the availability of large areas of pastures and barren and uncultivable waste lands used for grazing. In the irrigated tract, livestock pressure was comparatively less. It was 570 adult livestock units per 100 ha of permanent pastures in 1983. Due to decrease in livestock population of the irrigated tract, the pressure had decreased from 15% - 8% in all the land use categories during 1977-'83. Whereas due to increase in livestock population, pressure had increased from 33% to 36% in the pastoral tract; and more than half of in the rainfed tract during 1977-'83. The reasons of increase in density of livestock were found to be shrinkage of grazing lands due to cultivation of more and more marginal and sub-marginal lands, less fallowings, substitution of cattle with sheep and goats considered to be the most hardy livestock capable of surviving even on marginal and submarginal lands, etc.

In another study to understand the causes of shortage of grasses and shrubs in the arid regions, Bharara[20] recorded the villagers' expressed reasons. Of the various causes of shortage, increase in livestock was reported to be the most predominant cause of shortage of grasses which constituted 43 per cent of all the causes, followed by less land available for grazing (29%), less growth of grasses (7%), 6 per cent stoney land, 5 per cent and various others 3 per cent like attack of **Katra** (insect), growth of useless vegetation and less rainfall in all the tracts. Causes differed from tract to tract.

About the adequacy of the grazing grounds to feed the number of animals that used them, more than three fourths of the sampled households reported that the present grazing grounds were inadequate to feed the livestock. In a pastoral tract 74 per cent of the households expressed inadequacy of the present grazing grounds to meet the requirements of the livestock in the area. In a rainfed tract, 91 per cent of the house-holds expressed inadequacy of the present grazing grounds.

Irrational Land Use And Declining Grazing Resources

Many of the environmental problems today are due to the exponential growth of man's activities and technological developments. This is no less true in respect of irrational land use by mankind. Land here denotes the land, surface and all its characteristics which are of importance to man's existence and success. Against this background, the impact of irrational landuse on pastoral nomadism in arid districts of western Rajasthan may be examined.

The consideration of any form of landuse in West Rajasthan should be preceeded by an accurate assessment of the resources in dry land eco-system, their extent and distribution so that these could be harvested efficiently for productive exploitation towards total human welfare. This necessitates multi-disciplinary integrated surveys of natural resources[21]. The end product of integrated surveys is the generation of a proposed land utilization map which provide a clear picture of lands where livestock farming or pasturing can be undertaken.

Table 34 gives the present landuse in the districts of arid western Rajasthan for the period 1976-77 to 1980-81. The figures are collected from the revenue department of Government of Rajasthan. The average figures of the four years are taken into account. The table indicates that the highest percentage of land is under single crop. The **Permanent pasture or Oran** constitutes only 4.06%. But this is not the only unit that forms pasture grounds. Rocky and stony wastes, sandy wastes and long fallows also constitute grazing grounds. Thus the grazing ground available is about 41% - although about 7% of it (long fallow) are occasionally cultivated in long duration (4 to 5 years) - only in th years of very favourable rainfall. This secondary data only present the qualitative picture and don't show the extent of the pasture grounds.

Table 34: Present Landuse in arid Rajasthan (1976-77 to 1980-81)

	area in hectare	Percentage
Forest	285683	1.72
Settlement and Water Features	685659	3.29
Rocky waste & Stony waste	987579	4.74
Sandy waste (Cultivable waste)	5129338	24.63
Permanent pasture oran	846894	4.06
Orchards and plantations	28270	0.13
Cultivated lands		
Single cropped	9072278	43.68
Doubled cropped	805449	3.86
Long fallow	1542910	7.41
Short fallow	1393150	6.69
	20777210	100

Grazing ground: 8506721 ha or 40.84%

Cult. lands 12813787 ha or 61.64%

(including long fallow which is also grazing land.)

The degree and extent of landuse units can be best cartographed by means of field survey and remote sensing devises. Based on the intensity of survey, topographical maps - aerial photographs and landsat imagery interpretation, collection of field data and available informations, etc. three types of the landuse maps can be prepared from the restricting details viz., reconnaissance, detail reconnaissance and detail landuse maps. These are large sale maps being 1 : 100,000 to 1 : 50,000 1 : 25,000 and 1 : 15,000 or more in general in case of reconnaissance, detail reconnaissance or detail maps respectively. These maps show the extent and degree of landuse classes and thus depict the actual pattern of landuse (Fig. 13). These are helpful to delineate or find out problem areas, planning and execution works.

The present landuse and its relation to agricultural and livestock farming aspects can be best studied or geographically analysed by classifying the area into agro-climatic and agro-ecological regions. The arid zone of Rajasthan has earlier been classified into two macro and four micro agro-ecological regions (Table 35). The land use characteristics of these zones are also shown in Table 35.

Table 35: Agro-ecological and agro-climatic regions of Western Rajasthan

Macro Region		Micro region		Districts included	Area in Km and %
1.	Arid	1.	a. Kharif Mono-cropping.	Barmer, Jodhpur Churu, Jaisalmer, & Bikaner	133, 722 (64.20%)
		1.	b. Irrigated Kharif and Rabi cropping	Gangangar	20,764 (10%)
2.	Transitional hetric and arid and semi-arid	2.	a. Khair Mono-cropping	Jhunjhunu Sikar, and Nagaur	31,244 (15%)
		2.	b. Irrigated Kharif and Rabi cropping	Pali and Jalore	82,780 (10.80%)

Table 36 indicates that permanent pasture or Oran land, and waste lands including ten sub-classes primarily constitute the grazing ground. Besides the marginal lands where intensity of cultivated lands are less than 20% also comes under grazing ground during the drought years. Thus the actual pasture lands which form 46 per cent of the total area of western Rajasthan includes Oran, wastelands and marginal lands.

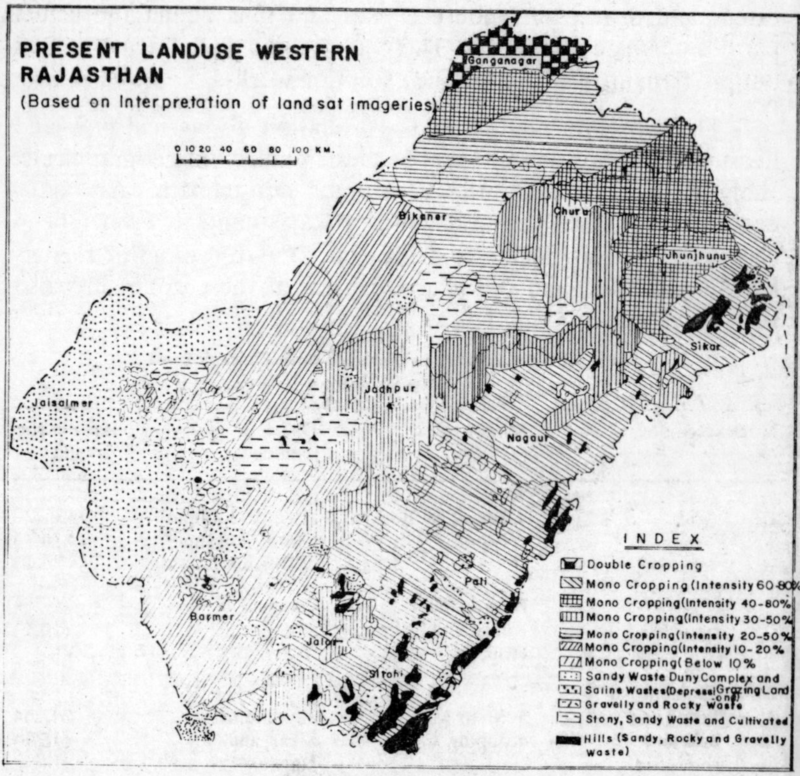

Fig. 13

Source : A.K. Sen & Balak Ram, 1988 Wasterland Development and their Utilisation, CAZRI, Jodhpur.

The availability of grazing ground in Western Rajasthan is quite high in comparison to national figure. In Western Rajasthan about 42% is available for grazing. The figure is above 50% in arid zone, while in Arid Kharif mono cropping belt more than 55% of the total area is available for livestock farming. In Jaisalmer,the available grazing ground exceeds 90%, while in Bikaner,it is above 60%. The low figure in Barmer and Churu is however due to the increased use of marginal lands for cultivation which however, is a menace to desertification and soil erosion. Same is the case with the districts of Nagaur, Sikar and Jhunjhunu. In Pali and Jodhpur districts saline waste accounts for the availability of more grazing ground[21].

The landuse pattern in arid region has traditionally been guided by the conservation-oriented motives. Recent trends, however, reveal that with the increasing intensity of land use the fragile balance between productivity and resource depletion process is gradually disappearing. The data on land utilization for the past 33 years reveal that consistent decadal increase was registered for forests, non-agricultural uses, permanent pastures and net sown area, whereas the same for culturable wastes, current and old fallows, and barren lands registered a considerable decline. Especially from increments in net sown areas, it can be concluded that areas which were hitherto incapable of raising crops and were serving as a valuable resource for livestock raising, were continuously going under the weight of plough. It is thus natural that depleted and degenerate landforms, when used to swell net cropped area would inevitably result into low and highly unstable production of crops under harsh xeric environment[22]. However long-term data do suggest that tendency to go in for short-run gains through irrational land use is retrogressive in terms of causing permanent damage to land resource base in the arid region. The existing land utilization norms, however, reveal that the rate of over-exploitation and thus misappropriation (Table 37) of marginal lands varies directly with aridity[23]. While in extremely arid district of Bikaner the over-exploitation accounts for 31% of the total cropped lands, the same accounts for about 20% for Jodhpur and only 12% for Nagaur districts. It is thus obvious that irrationality in the existing land utilization pattern is mainly due to a combination of subsistence motivation, risk diversion strategy and increased efficiency of market signals.

Table 36: Pasture grounds in Western Rajasthan

District		Total area in hectare	Pasture lands in ha & $ Permanent pasture Oran	Waste	Marginal	Total
1A.	Jodhpur	2217800	133500	682790	271650	1087940
			(6.02)	(30.79)	(12.25)	(49.06)
	Bikaner	2885072	26597	1417020	294380	1737997
			(0.92)	(49.12)	(10.20)	(60.24)
	Jaisalmer	4135700	145408	3634723	3021	3783152
			(13.42)	(87.88)	(0.08)	(91.48)
	Churu	1685114	49261	57100	102143	208504
			(2.92)	(3.39)	(6.1)	(12.37)
Total Arid Monocropping		13740980	569232	6293608	690479	7553319
			(4.14)	(45.90)	(5.02)	(55.06)
1b.	Gangangar	2041446	25910	301451	38792	386353
			(1.27)	(14.77)	(3.0)	(19.04)
Total arid		15782426	595142	6595059	6729171	7919672
			(3.77)	(41.78)	(4.62)	(50.18)
2a.	Sikar	774925	48200	71044	1889	121130
			(6.22)	(9.17)	(0.24)	(15.63)
	Jhunjhunu	592730	44589	249224	1826	71339
			(7.53)	(4.20)	(0.03)	(12.03)
	Nagaurr	1768011	80400	84600	19283	184283
			(4.55)	(4.78)	(1.1)	(10.43)
Total Transitional Monocropping		3135666	173189	180565	143602	497356
			(5.53)	(5.76)	(4.60)	(15.86)
2b	Jalore	1056357	51139	96709	956	148504
			(4.84)	(9.15)	(0.06)	(14.05)
	Pali	1229762	92463	178144	19962	290569
			(7.52)	(14.49)	(1.62)	(23.63)
Total Transition Kharif & Rabi Cropping		228619	143602	274853	20618	439073
			(6.28)	(12.02)	(0.90)	(12.20)
Total Transitional Arid & Semi-Arid		5421785	316791	455418	164220	936429
			(5.84)	(8.40)	(3.03)	(17.2)
Total W. Rajasthan		21204211	911933	7050477	893691	8856101
			(4.30)	(33.25)	(4.21)	(41.76)

Another dimension of the irrationality in land utilization is reflected in the skewed distribtion of cropped lands in arid region. From the results presented by two censuses of operational holdings in the arid region of Western Rajasthan it is observed that in 1970-71, 51% of the small holdings occupied only 13% of total cultivated area and only about 11% of large holdings accounted for as much as 50% of area. The situation did not substantially change in 1976-77. For, 48% of small holdings still accounted for only about 12% of cultivated area as against 10% of very large holdings occupying as much as 40% of the total cultivated area. The impact of land reforms on pattern of redistribution could only be seen in shifts from very large to medium holdings.

Table 37 : Misappropriation of land-use capacities in arid areas of western Rajasthan

Area survey	Annual average rain-fall (mm)	Total area (km2)	Cultivable area by land-use capability survey classes I to V (%)	Cultivated/ Cultivable area by re-venue records (%)	Total exploita-tion of marginal lands (%)
Chohtan Block	220	3,164	32	63	31
Saila Block	320	1,455	64	86	22
Bikaner Distt	250	21,336	49	85	36
Jalore Block	360	932	76	83	7
Jodhpur Distt	360	22,860	63	83	20
Negaur Distt	390	17,643	75	87	12

Source : Kolarkar, A.S. 1984, Significance of agro-forestry programmes as indicated by land-use capability surveys in arid region. In Agro-forestry in Arid and Semi-arid Zones, CAZRI Publication No. 24, Central Arid Zone Research Institute, Jodhpur.

Further, most of the surplus lands available for distribution belonged to the categories of marginal and sub- marginal lands with unsurmountable constraints in the availability and control of resources including technology and knowledge inputs[24]. **The land distribution thus essentially turned out to be a handle in hands of small and medium farmers for accentuating the pace of land resource degradation.**

Further, sub-optimality of land uşe can be attributed to an astonishing consistency in pattern of allocation of cropped area among principal crops in arid regions of western Rajasthan. Year after year, same cropped area with fragile productive base has been distributed between major Kharif crops leading to further deterioration in land productivity and frequent crop failure.

Decline of Common Property Resources

From the early 1950's to early 1980s, the following common property resources in the arid zone declined in area and deteriorated in quality.

Grazing lands

Village forests, permanent pastures, uncultivable and cultivable wastelands, and croplands fallowed for longer periods broadly constitute the total grazing area in the villages. This area is supplemented by cropland in the post-crop season when anyone can graze his animals there. Table 38 provides relevant information on all other grazing areas. The proportions of common property resources used for grazing in the total land area of the study villages is fast declining.

Significantly the decline in area of common property resources was greater during the decade preceding 1963-64 than in succeedings years. This was the peak period of land reforms in the region. Forests and permanent pastures, which were already small in area, declined the most. The fallow lands declined mainly through a fall in long-fallow rotation.

The trends in the decline of common property resources are also evident for the arid zone as a whole. Land utilization trends for all 11 districts comprising the arid zone of western Rajasthan are shown in Table 39. The common property resources (grazing aras) in the region have been declining consistently since 1951-52. Again, the decline was greatest during 1951-52 to 1961-62.

One consequence of the decline in grazing space is the increase in density of animals per unit of common grazing land. In the arid zone as a whole,the density of livestock expressed in terms of animal units increased from 39 animals units per 100 hectares of grazing land in 1951-52 to 105 during 1977-78.

Table 38 : Changes in Common Grazing Areas as % of Total Area In Six Villages of Western Rajasthan

	Percent of total area in study villages									
	Nagaur				Jodhpur				Jaisalmer	
Grazing area	1953-54	1963-64	1972-73	1977-78	1953-54	1963-64	1972-73	1977-78	1953-54	1963-64
Forests Permanent	2	1	0	0	3	2	2	2	0	0
Pastures Uncultivable	6	3	1	1	7	3	3	3	3	1
Wastelands Cultivable	17	13	12	11	13	10	10	9	38	35
Wastelands	18	10	7	6	15	7	4	3	26	12
Fallow lands (Other than current fallows)	15	10	8	6	18	13	10	9	16	13

Table 39: Changes in Characteristics of Common Property Resources in Western Rajasthan, 1951-78

Characteristic	1951-52	1961-62	1971-72	1977-78
Area (million ha)	11.3	9.8	9.2	8.7
Area as percent of total geo-raphic area	60.5	51.1	47.9	45.1
Percent decline in CPR area over previousperiod	–	12.4	6.7	4.5
Livestock per 100 ha of CPR's (no. of animal units)	39	86	94	105
Population per sq.km in the zone	30	39	51	N.A.

Note : Common property resources include forests, permanent pastures, uncultivable wastelands, and fallow lands other than current fallows.

Private croplands : Seasonal common property resources

Public grazing on private croplands in the post- crop season is an important informal arrangement helping stock raisers. Because of this practice of periodic common access, the cropped area could be described as seasonal common property resources. Depending upon crop and soil moisture conditions, the available forage consists of crop leftovers, undergrowth, resprouting of harvested crops, and bushes. The net sown area in the arid region as a whole has increased from about 6.6 million hectares in 1956-57 to 8.3 million hectares during 1977-78. Despite an increase of about 25 percent in the seasonal common property resources for grazing, their contribution to total forage supplies for grazing seems to have declined in recent years. The large scale introduction of tractors has meant that soil preparation for the next season is finished soon after the harvest of the previous crop. This deprives the animals of any post-harvest grazing. Use of tractors has also led to a decline in the grazing available from long fallows, cultivable wastes, and the like, because tractors are not subject to the constraint a very short wet period imposes on soil preparation by draft animals - a constraint that in the past restricted cropping to a limited area[25].

Causes Of The Decline

The decline of common property resources is a result of multiple forces. It is often not easy to measure the role of specific factors in this process. However, a description of the circumstances influencing people's action can shed light on the relative roles of different factors. Two factors that seem to have contributed significantly to the decline of common property resources in the arid zone are: (1) land reforms during the early 1950s; and (2) population growth.

Land Reforms

The tenurial situation on the eve of the formation of the Rajasthan State in 1949 was characterized by a variety of formal and informal arrangements governing the control and use of lands in different princely states. There was a variety of intermediaries - for example, **jagirdar, biswedar, muafidar, rajvi,** and rack-renting and tenurial uncertainties were common. The early land legislation of the State was designed to regulate rents, protect tenants and finally abolish the intermediaries. The actual tillers of the land were made landowners and brought into direct contact with the State. Further, vast areas of submarginal lands were distributed as private holdings for cultivation under the various legislations, in particular the

Rajasthan Land Revenue (Allotment of Land for Agricultural Purposes) Rules 1957. However, while making the tenants owners of the land as well as distributing new lands to private land-holders, the State did not give any consideration to the use capability of the land. Nor did it impose any obligation on the beneficiaries regarding use or conservation. In other words, with regard to ownership, agrarian legislation in Rajasthan (except for the land ceiling laws) treated the desert lands or submarginal lands in arid areas on a par with the lands in well endowed areas of the southern and southeastern parts of the State.

No land legislation dealt specifically with the determination and regulation of the use intensity of land. The **Rajasthan Tenancy (Government) Rules 1955** and the **Rajasthan Land Revenue Act 1956** contain some provisions for the regulation of land use, but their approach is entirely different from what has been described above. They merely stipulate that it is the duty of the revenue officials to ensure that a given piece of land is put to the same use to which according to the revenue records it was put in the past. Thus, through the above laws, the State attempts to regulate the use of the land according to the revenue records and not according to its physically desirable level of use intensity. In effect this procedure tends to perpetuate the existing maladjustments in the land use pattern.

Indeed, the **Rajasthan Agricultural Lands Utilisation Act 1954** goes a step further. The traditional practice of rotating, cropping and fallowing is a compromise between the intensive and extensive type of land use in the arid area. But the above Act (Sectionl 4) completely ignoring the traditional wisdom of the desert farmer, empowers,the district collector to prohibit the fallowing of the croplands. If the landowner fails to cultivate the land and obstructs the alternative arrangements for cultivation made by the collector he is liable to penalty up to Rs. 500 per case. Though no cases of implementation of this provision have been noted, the law itself illustrates the government's disregard of the nature of the problem of arid lands.

The economy of the arid region, in general, and its north-western parts, in particular, is dominated by livestock farming. Practically every village had some common pasture lands. **But the**

State has no legislation reflecting its concern for these grazing lands and there is no coherent pasture policy. The State Government, through certain provisions of the **Rajasthan Panchayat (General) Rules 1955,** has shifted the responsibility for pasture developement and management to the village panchayat (council). The panchayats have neither technical competence nor political and administrative power to introduce any measure to regulate stocking rates, grazing rights, or rotational grazing. An evaluation study revealed that not a single panchayat had taken up any step to manage or develop village pastures and forests. Thus, as in the past, the utilization of grazing lands is governed by informal institutional arrangement under which uncontrolled and unrestricted grazing, without any obligations to the grazing land is the rule.

Policies related to land tenure emerged as part of the land reform programmes in the State during the 1950s. The primary objective of land reforms was to replace the feudal agrarian structure by a more equitable and just agrarian system in keeping with the ideals of a democratic state. The feudal agrarian order, which had developed over a long period in the princely states of Rajasthan, had a number of exploitative features. The production, distribution and exchange relations between the landowner and the land-user were exploitative. The land use pattern it encouraged was not related to the land use capabilities and hence was already over-explolitative. The land reforms were only concerned with the exploitative features of the feudual order, as they related to the tillers of the land, and not to the land itself. Thus the need for preventing very intensive use of land was completely overlooked, and the conservation needs of the resource base never figured in the land reform laws. Indeed, the real consequence of agrarian reforms through the distribution of additional submarginal lands has been to accentuate the process of over-exploitation[26].

The introduction of land reforms during the early 1950s constituted a major institutional intervention. The reforms encouraged the privatization of common property resources for use as croplands; drastically reduced the private cost of cultivating submarginal lands (including common property resources); and dismantled the traditonal arrangements that protected and regulated the use of common property resources.

Prior to the introduction of land reforms, the fedual landlord was the sole custodian or "owner" of the village lands. All farmers except his kinsmen were the landldord's tenants. They paid substantial rent in kind (one fourth to one-half of farm produce) for land they cultivated. Although the common property resources belonged to the landlord, villagers had access to them in return for certain charges. While a fixed proportion of land revenue from cultivated land went as payment to the state ruler, revenue from the common property resources went to the landlord's own exchequer.

Methods of revenue generation from common property resources included a fixed grazing tax per head of animal; the auctioning of produce; a number of different levies on users; and penalties for violation of regulations. The number of different levies and taxes imposed in princely State of Jodhpur in 1941 varied from 50 to 150, of which 64 were considered legitimate by an enquiry committee appointed by the ruler of the state. Many related to common property resources. Through levies and penalties on the use of common property resources, the landlord exploited the peasants. However, as a byproduct of this exploitative mechanism emerged a management system that protected, maintained, and regulated use of common property resources.

Following land reforms the Jagirdari system was abolished. Peasants were made owners of the lands they formerly cultivated as tenants. The land revenue tax payable annually to the government on these lands was drastically reduced. Vast areas of common property resources, mostly submarginal lands unsuited to cultivation, were distributed as croplands to the landless as well as to those who already had land. Within a decade of land reforms, in the arid region as a whole,3.4 million hectares of common property resources were transferred to private ownership for the purpose of arable farming. This meant an increase of nearly 50 per cent in the land put under the plough in the arid zone. It also meant a decline of between 7 and 26 per cent in common property resources for grazing.

The custodianship of the remaining common property resources was transferred to the village community, represented by village Panchayats (elected councils). The provision of common access continued as in the past, but the old system of management of common property resources disappeared. The village Panchayats did not impose grazing taxes and levies on users, despite being legally empowered to do so. The maintenance and upkeep of common property resources suffered as the Panchayats depended more and more on assistance from the government for this purpose. The main reason for the ineffectiveness of Panchayats, despite their domination by exfeudal landlords in some cases, is that they were neither as authoritarian as Jagirdars, nor bold enough to take hard decisions (such as imposing taxes) that would displease their voters.

Over exploitation and depletion of common property resources resulted largely because there was (and remains) no private cost to using these resources. Estimates based on detailed investigations in some villages of Nagaur district indicate that prior to land reforms the animal grazer had to pay Rs. 41 per household in cash or kind (at 1976-77 prices) plus Rs. 1.25 grazing tax per animal per year (at 1976-77 prices). After the land reforms this cost was reduced to zero.

Population Growth

Increased population pressure is widely considered an important contributor to shrinkage and depletion of common property resources. In the case of the arid zone of Rajasthan, however, the role of population in the decline of common property resources does not appear to be dominant. Although no long-term records are available, scattered and circumstantial evidence supports this view.

Privatization of common property resources in the arid zone has invariably meant conversion of common property resources land into cropland. Hence, the impact of population growth can be judged in terms of increase in the area of cropland as well as the decline in the extent of common property resources. The population of the arid zone increased by 29.8 percent from 1951 to 1961 and by 27.9 per cent from 1961 to 1971. Croplands increased by 50 percent and 7 percent respectively during the same periods. The area of common property resources declined by around 16 percent and 7 percent respectively.

Demographic factors in the post-land reforms phase: The introduction of land reforms unleashed the forces of population growth. The land reforms of the early 1950's not only liberally distributed submarginal lands to the people, they also changed the economics of land use. Land was granted to people for nominal annual rents payable to the government. In Nagaur district, rent payable as crop share to the Hagirdar was Rs. 16 per hectare (at 1976-77 prices); following land reforms, fixed rent on submarginal lands was Rs. 11.50 per hectare. The low fixed rent reflected the low crop productivity of these lands. The reduced cost of submarginal lands, accompanied by the government's liberal approach to their distribution, induced people to acquire private lands at the cost of common property resources.

Changes in the occupational structure of villages also increased dependence on, and therefore demand for, cropland. The **Jajmani** system governing patron-client relationships had tied many rural households to their traditional caste occupation (services and crafts). This system was disrupted following the introduction of the land reforms. Dependence on traditonal caste occupations now appeared less economically attractive than farming land available for a very nominal charge. Subsidies, credit, and other forms of assistance available mainly to land owners were further incentives to land ownership. This induced traditionally noncultivating households to acquire cropland. During the feudal period, an important category of absentee landlords consisted of land owners from the Rajput caste who worked in the military forces of princely states. With the merger of princely states in the Indian Union during 1950-52, most of these army units were disbanded. These people returned to find their lands already transferred to their tenants. The rehabilitation of these and other absentee landlords who lost lands during the reforms again led to distribution of lands once held as common property.

As these examples illustrate, demographic factors have exerted increased pressure on common property resources laregly through the opportunities for cultivation created by various provision of the land reforms programme[27].

Technical innovation: The introduction of irrigation, fertilizers, and improved seed varieties has affected a few parts of the arid zone. The most important technological change influencing common property, however, was the widespread introduction of tractors. The introduction was initially supported by government subsidies to farmers and subsequently gained momentum due to its commercial profitability. For the region as a whole, the number of tractors almost tripled, from 2,251 in 1961 to 6,652 in 1971, and it has increased further since then. In the study of the arid zone, Jodha[28] found that in a cluster of six villages the number of tractors increased from 10 in 1964-65 to 59 in 1973-74, and the proportion of cropped area to total land area increased from 44 percent to 81 percent.

The soils of the region are mainly sandy and prone to wind erosion unless protected by a vegetation cover. Therefore, diminution or removal of this cover due to cultivation has certainly accelerated the process of wind erosion. This situation has worsened further with the gradual decline in fallow farming (Fig.14). Whereas only a few years ago in the districts of Jodhpur, Barmer, and Bikaner, the farmers used to keep half of their land under fallow, now this figure has come to less than thirty per cent. Thus the productive effect of vegetation, which would naturally come during fallow period, has lessened. The problem has got further aggravated by the disc ploughing of land.

Post-Independence land reforms coupled with agricultural production drives have resulted into a continuous forced-conversion of wastelands into cropped lands. During last 30 years, barren lands from the 6 districts (Bikaner, Barmer, Jhunjhunu, Nagaur, Pali and Sikar), culturable wastes from all arid districts excepting Barmer and Jaisalmer districts,and long fallows in all elevan arid districts excepting Sri Ganganagar have declined resulting into increased cropping area. It is, thus natural that such a tendency would naturally lead to increase in uncertainty-oriented crop production. Another noteworthy damage that this would cause is on the traditional economic advantage of livestock farming in the region. Arid region of Western Rajasthan is eminently suitable for production of milk, meat, bullocks, wool and other livestock products which are predominantly based on the extensive grazing systems in the arid wastelands. Once the flow of reduction in area is accentuated due to pressure of human population in favour of cultivation, the added geometrical annual growth of about 2.5 percent per annum would have to thrive increasingly on limited area with declining livestock productivity. If continued unabated,

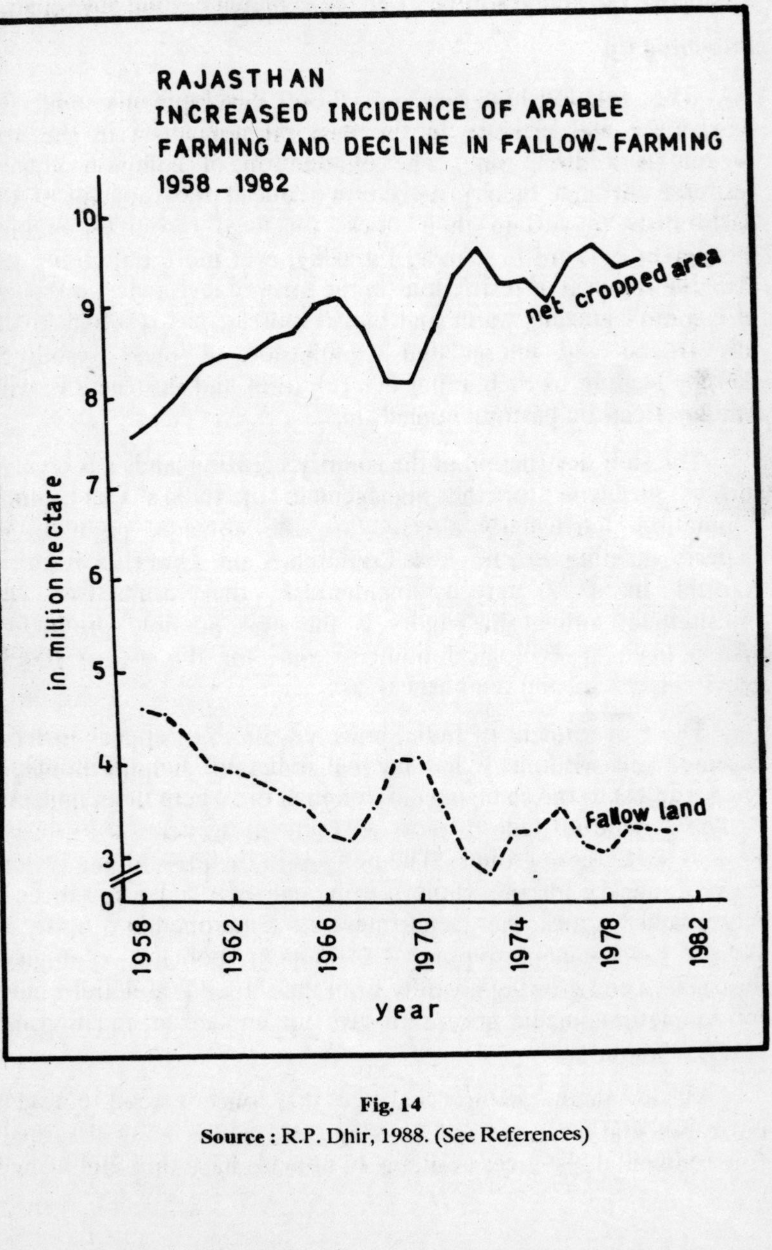

Fig. 14

Source : R.P. Dhir, 1988. (See References)

the increase in livestock number coupled with decline in livestock based allocation of wastelands and continuous cropping on wasteland, the land resource would be depleted beyond any repair[29].

Summing Up

The relationship between these developments and the persistence and increase in the pastoral nomadism in the arid regions is a direct one. The elimination of common grazing resource through their privitization reduced the capacity of the pastoralists to sustain their flocks on local resources, making movement outward in search of grazing, ever more imperative. So also, the removal of restrictions in the form of levies etc. on the use of common grazing, water and fuel resources, has resulted in the unrestricted and unregulated exploitation of these resources, thereby leading to their rapid deterioration and destruction, with similar effects on pastoral nomadism.

The slow destruction of the country's grazing lands has created serious problems for the management of India's vast animal population. Particularly affected are the nomadic populations. Experts meeting at the UN Conference on Desertification in Nairobi in 1977 agreed unanimously that nomadism and transhumant animal husbandry is the best possible productive system from an ecological point of view for the use of fragile ecoystems in arid and semi-arid areas.

The Government of India, however, does not appear to have accepted this wisdom. It has no real policy for helping nomadic groups adjust to the changing environment or to help them improve it. The general attitude of most government agencies is to devise ways to settle these groups. "The nomads in the present day society prove a menace for the whole society and their sedenterisation is inescapable," states the Department of Environemnt's State of India's Environment report. Government policies, ecological destruction and growing hostility from the settled populations have forced many nomadic groups to give up nomadism and become landless labourers.

Meanwhile,the natural balance that once existed between environmental resources and stocking rates is now being disturbed. Environmental resources available to nomads have thus diminished noticeably because of inadequate government policies to protect grazing lands and active government policies to push crop production on marginal lands. To ensure their own survival livestock breeders have responded by increasing their animal populations and keeping more browsers. The result is heavier destruction of grazing lands and pressure on forests. The government, therefore, faces its biggest challenge in determining the future development strategy for its nomadic groups and in restoring the country's grazing lands to health. But politicians at all levels- from state chief ministers to union cabinet ministers-have no understanding of the problems of nomads and would prefer them dead and gone[30].

The answer to the huge problem of fodder lies in an appropriate and integrated national land-use plan. So far most attention has been paid to the area under cultivation. But nearly 50 per cent of the land area is uncultivated and most is uncultivable. India has not yet evolved any policies or programmes for its upkeep and proper maintenance except stray, occasional and disconnected efforts. The hard fact is that the management of forest lands, grazing lands and croplands cannot be isolated from each other[31].

REFERENCES

1. R.K. Tyagi and Panjab Sing, 1988, Grazing Resources and Grazing Systems in India, in (ed) **Pasture and Forage Crops Research - A State of Knowledge report, Third International Rangelands Congress,** New Delhi, India, IGFRI, Jhansi.
2. Ibid.
3. Vinod Shankar, Suresh Kumar, etal, 1988, Grazing Resources of Semi-arid and Arid Regions In the (ed) **Pasture and Forage Crops Research - A State of Knowledge report, Third International Rangelands Congress,** New Delh, India, IGFRI,Jhansi.
4. Rekib, A. 1981 Some aspects of Livestock feeding on herbages in Bundelkhand (U.P.). Paper presented at **National Seminar on Rainfed Agriculture and Farm Forestry with Special Reference to Bundelkhand Region** held at IGFRI, Jhansi during December 17 - 19, 1981.
5. Raheja, PC 1966 Rajasthan desert can bloom with forage **Indian Farming** 15:47
6. Shankar, Vinod and Suresh Kumar, 1987. Grazing Resources of Jaisalmer : **Ecology and Developmental Planning with Special Reference to Sewan Grasslands.** Pub. No. 28, CAZRI, Jodhpur.
7. Op.cit, Vinod Shankar, Suresh Kumar etal.
8. Shankarnarayan, K.A and Shankar Vinod, 1984. Grasses and Legumes for Forage and Soil Conservation. ICAR, New Delhi. Singh, M. and R.P. Singh. 1986 **Effect of fodder and grain legume intercrops and the quality of** Cenchrus Ciliurislinn, **Indian J.Agri Socie.,** 56:704- 709.

9. Mann, H.S., S.P. Malhotra and K.A. Shankarnarayan. 1977. Land and Resource Utilisation in the Arid Zone. In **Desertification and its Control.** ICAR NEW DELHI.

10. Gupta, R.K and S.K. Saxena. 1966 Habitat, grassland types and forage potential of Jalore district in Western Rajasthan. **Ann. Arid Zone** 14:245-250.

11. Op.cit Shankar Vinod and Suresh Kumar

12. Shankarnarayan, K.A and J.C. Kalla 1985. **Management Systems for Natural Vegetation in Arid and Semi-Arid Areas** CAZRI, Jodhpur - 132 pp.

13. Ahuja, L.D - Livestock Production in Arid Rangelands (unpublished paper)

14. Bharara, L.P. 1988. Socio-economic and cultural requisites of rangelands technology and constraints in its adoption in arid zone of Rajasthan. In **Rangelands Resource and Management**, Range Management Society of India, IGFRI, Jhansi.

15. Mudgal, R.D. and Beniwal - Pasture development and utilization to minimise the sheep migration from arid region of Rajasthan (unpublished paper).

16. Op.cit. Shankarnarayan, K.A and J.C. Kalla (1985).

17. Dhir, R.P. 1988. Flux in the Indian arid zone, **In Desert Ecology**, Scientific Publishers, Jodhpur.

18. Kavoori, P.S. - **Pastoral Transhumance in Western Rajasthan : A Report on the Migratory system of Sheep IDS**, Jaipur.

19. Bharara, L.P. 1988 Animal Human Relationship and Desertification in Arid Zone, In **Desertification, Monitoring and Control**, Scientific Publishers, Jodhpur.

20. Op. Cit, Bharara, L.P. (1988).

21. Sen, A.K. 1988 Livestock Farming - A Form of Land Use in W. Rajasthan, In **Desert Ecology**, Scientific Publishers, Jodhpur.

22. Malhotra, S.P and J.C. Kalla 1990. Social and Economic Constraints in optimal Land use under Arid Conditions In Technologies for Wasteland.

23. Kolarkar, A.S. 1984. Singificance of Agro- forestry programme as indicated by land use capacity surveys in arid region. In **Agro- forestry in Arid and Semi-arid Zones.** CAZRI, Pub. No. 24, Jodhpur.

24. Jodha, N.S. 1977 Land Tenure Problems and Policies in Arid Region of Rajasthan. **In Desertification and its Control.** ICAR, New Delhi pp . 335 - 47.

25. – – – 1986.The Decline of Common Property Resources In Rajasthan, India. **Pastoral Development Network** Paper 22C, Sept. '86. ODI, London.

26. – – – 1982. The Role of Administration in Desertification. Land Tenure as a Factor in the Historical Ecology of Western Rajasthan. In **Desertification and Development. Dry land Ecology In Social Perspective,** Academic Press, London.

27. – – – – (1986)

28. Ibid.

29. Kalla, J.C. 1988 Criteria of Economic Evaluation of Wasteland Development Programmes. In **Wasteland Development and their Utilization**, Scientific Publishers, Jodhpur.

30. The State of India's Environment (1984-85). The Second Citizen's Report. **Centre for Science & Environment, New Delhi 1985.**

31. Ibid.

5

Patterns of Pastoral Nomadism

The sheep and wool industry has flourished in dry areas as agriculture in these regions is either uncertain or difficult. Sheep raising has been wedged into agriculture, mostly by grazing the animals on the stubbles. Droughts are frequent in the dry areas and when the crops fail altogether, the farmer can still count on the income from the sale of wool and surplus stock. Therefore, sheep raising contributes substantially to the income of the farmers in these areas. About 40 per cent of the rural population, in the arid zone depends on animal husbandry, particularly sheep raising, and an equally large proportion depends on this indirectly.

Sheep in India are mostly owned by nomads or semi-nomadic people who constantly move their flocks in search of good pastures and water. There are certain nomadic communities like **Raika** and **Rabari** whose main occupation is sheep rearing. Sheep farming is a hereditary occupation with these people.

Pastoral nomadism in arid zones is primarily sheep- goat pastoralism. There is an extremely close and delicate relation between this type of adaptation and the environmental milieu in which it operates, and this relationship also creates the basic necessity for mobility. The reason for this close relationship lies both, in nature of the environment as also in certain features inherent in the subsistence technique. Thus the very limitations of the environment excercise care in its exploitation, the fundamental factor of aridity creating a relaively low threshold of utilization. On the other side too, i.e. in terms of technology, sheep and goat have an extremely high rate of grazing, thus continued pasturing in one locality cannot be done. These two factors of environment and technology provide thus the basic thrust for nomadism.

Sheep are essentially dependent on pastures and therefore the sheep flocks of the arid region remain more or less under migration all through the year in search of water, feed and fodder as the availability of of grazing resources, including the top feeds, in the arid and semi-arid regions are unable to sustain the flocks. The arid area is extended in 12 out of 27 districts of Rajasthan. The annual rainfall in the area varies between 16.0 cms in Jaisalmer to 45.54 cms in Sikar. The arid area is spread in about 1.96 lakh (1 lakh = 100,000) sq. kms. It has sheep population of 70.50 lakhs, out of these about 37 per cent i.e., 27.16 lakhs sheep remain under migration to different places. The sheep flocks of the districts having lowest annual rainfall like Jaisalmer, Barmer and Bikaner (between 16.0 to 27.72 cm) have migration rate of 55.53 to 59.84 per cent whereas the sheep flocks of the districts such as Pali, Azmer and Sikar which have relatively higher rainfall of 41.53 to 45.54 cms have migration rate ranging from 13.05 to 31.99 per cent. It has been observed that rate of sheep migration is negatively correlated with the average rainfall in the district (r=0.638). These details are given in Table 40. It has also been observed that with every one cm reduction in average rainfall of the district the migration rate increased by 1.11 per cent.[1]

Seasonal migration of sheep from their native home tracts to places where there is sufficient water and grass in the fields is an important feature of sheep management in the arid zones. There are very few sheep breeders who have their own pastures and, hence, a vast majority of the pastoralists graze their sheep and other pack animals like camels, donkeys on grazing areas owned by the government, forest department and the agriculturists. A survey conducted by the Institute of Agricultural Research Statistics on the estimation of wool production in the arid areas of Rajasthan and Gujarat revealed that in the Joria region of Gujarat State (1964-65) 66.4 Per cent of the sheep flockowners had no land and 17.8 per cent had land upto 3.2 hectares each. Similarly, in Rajasthan (1960-61) the survey revealed, that 4.9 per cent of the sheep flockowners were landless and 41.5 per cent had 4 hectares or less.[2] Another survey on "sheep rearing and wool production in India : Problems and Prospects" conducted by the Indian Institute of Management, Ahmedabad during 1982-83 revealed that in Gujarat 54.0 per cent sheep flockowners were landless and 18.0 per cent had land between 2.5 ha. to 4 ha. whereas in Rajasthan 17.0 per cent were landless 26.0 per cent had land between 1 ha. to 2 ha.[3]

Table 40 : Average Annual Rainfall and Sheep Migration in the Arid Districts of Rajsthan

District	Average rainfall	Sheep Population (lakhs) (1988)	No.of Average Sheep migrated (Lakhs) (83-90)	Percentage of sheep migrated
Jaisalmer	16.0	4.84	2.75	56.85
Bikaner	26.37	8.23	4.93	59.84
Ganganagar	25.37	5.37	0.86	16.13
Barmer	27.74	4.82	2.67	55.53
Jodhpur	31.87	7.69	3.71	48.26
Churu	32.35	5.05	1.78	35.31
Nagaur	38.86	9.27	3.33	35.90
Jhunjhunu	40.43	2.12	0.68	31.84
Jalore	40.44	4.20	1.59	37.92
Pali	41.53	10.31	3.29	31.99
Ajmer	43.96	5.67	1.10	20.92
Sikar	45.54	2.93	0.38	13.05
Overall	34.21	70.50	27.16	36.96

$(r = -0.638)^{**}_{2.5}$ $(b= -1.108)^{**}_{5.1}$

** Significant at P 0.01 level

The managemental practices of the sheep in the arid regions of Rajasthan depends on factors such as intensity of cultivation, land holdings of the farmers, fallow land available, range land for grazing, rainfall during the season, and other lands available for grazing. At present, during the larger part of the year sheep are raised on stubbles. Stubbles grazing is nàtaurally available in abundance in areas where land is fallow after the **Kharif** crop. In the plains, sheep,therefore, migrate to these fallow lands.

The grazing management of sheep, which ultimately influences the pattern of pastoral nomadism, in the arid areas may be broadly classified in to three categories, (1) **rainy season grazing management, (2) winter grazing management, and (3) summer grazing management.**

Rainy Season Grazing Management

During rainy season the grazing management of sheep in rural areas depends on the size of land holdings and cultivated lands. A type of rotational grazing is practised in the districts of Jaisalmer, Barmer and Bikaner where rainfall is less than 30 cm per annum and less area is used for crops and more area is available for the grazing of sheep. The different types of grasses on which sheep feed during July to September-October are **(i) sewan (Lasiurus sindicus). (ii) bhurrat (Cenchrus biflourus), (iii) gynthil (Dactylocterium sindicum), (iv) tantia (Eleusine compressa) (v) karad (Dicanthium annulatum), (vi) murat (Panicum turgidum), (vii) dhaman (Cenchurs ciliaris), (viii) kaladhaman (Cenchrus setigerus), (ix) lapda (Arisfida sp.), (x) bakaria (Indigofera cordifolia) and (xi) gramna (Panicum antidotale).** The grazing land in these districts is abundant and animals thrive well on these desertic grasses.

Individual land holding are also large in these districts. The farmer keeps his flock moving in his field, and in **gochar** and other community grazing areas. Vegetable material in wool is more during the October clip, particularly **bhurrat** due to abundance of growth of grasses. **Jaisalmeri, Mogra, Pugal and Marwari** breeds of sheep from border districts are mainly managed in these three districts. Whenever the rainfall is low the grass coverage of the area decreases resulting in migration of flocks. The **Marwari** sheep are migratory in nature. They migrate every year to the adjoining districts of Panjab, Haryana, Uttar Pradesh, Gujarat and Madhya Pradesh. About 1.5 million sheep migrate every year from rural areas of Rajasthan, out of which 0.5 million are permanent migratory sheep (Report on migration of Sheep, 1979). Migratory sheep are normally managed on the ravines of **Chambal,** jungles of Madhya Pradesh and on stubbles after the harvesting of **rabi** crops.

In the districts of Nagaur, Pali, Jodhpur and Sirohi the rainfall is between 30 and 40 cm but very little grazing land is available since more land is under agricultural crops. The sheep are kept on **talab, gochar, jor, beers** and **orans.** Small area of land is kept uncultivated for the grazing of sheep along with cows, buffaloes and camels. The sheep farmer migrates his flock to the adjoining districts of Bikaner, Jaisalmer and Barmer, even during rainy season from July to October. There is a system of gelagrazing in which the flock of sheep graze on the grasses and even crops in the vicinity of the road while pretending to migrating his sheep to other areas by the shepherds. Sometimes such grazing creates law and order problem. Very few farmers having small flock of 25-35 sheep resort to such method of grazing.

Jhunjhunu, Sikar, Churu and Gangangar are the districts where very little grazing land is available for sheep flock even during rainy season. Hence the animals are kept on small plots of land left for grazing. During rainy season the flocks are kept on a small piece of grazing land leading to high carrying capacity with low availability of nutrient to the animals.

The sheep in the district of Nagaur, Churu, Sikar and Jhunjhunu migrate to adjoining districts particulary in the **Magra** region — that is **Kolayat** and farther towards Rajasthan Canal area even during July to September months. The animals are brought back during October-November when after harvesting the stubble of the **kharif** crop (bhelwar) is available for sheep grazing.

Winter Grazing Management

Sheep farmers mostly keep their sheep on the harvested fields of **moth, guar, bajra, till, moong** and **chawal** in these districts. The **pala (Ziziphus nummularia), bant, murali (Mimosa hamata)** and other dry grasses of the desert provide nutrient to the sheep. Some sheep farmers provide **loong** to the sheep (the leaves of **prosopis cineraria)** to the pregnant and lactaing sheep and young lambs during winter to keep the flock in good health.

Summer Grazing Management

From March to June the sheep flocks mostly depend on the grasses which start to grow during March, e.g. **dachhab, dab and**

sewan. But the shrubs such as **Fog (Callygonum polygonoides)** khimp **(Leptodenia sparticum, ker (Capparis decidua), kumat (Acaeciasenegal) murali (Mimosa lamata), kikar (AScacea nilotica), aak (Calotropis procera), sinia (Crotalaria burhia), bui (Aerua tomentosa and munja (Saccharum munja) are utilised by** the sheep.[4] During March the **phog** flowers(**phogla**) provide good feed along wite **dacchhab** which grows on the sand-dunes. During April the ripe flowers of **phog** locally known as **jhintal** provide good feeding as other grasses are not available during summer to sheep flock. The **lassu,** the green branches of **phog,** are also eaten by sheep apart from **khimp, bui, pala, bant, kankera, murali, kumat, aak and sinia** which also grow during this period of the year. Good winter rains provide better pasture during this period.[5]

Sheep Breed and Migration

The major sheep breeds of the arid area and their distribution are presented in Table-41. The sheep of arid area are known to possess quality wool most suitable for carpet manufacture. The **Chokla** breed produce finer type wool and have shown potentials to be improved as a fine wool breed. The wool from **Magra** sheep is ideal carpet type and is the only known Indian breed to possess lustre. The **Pugal** is hardy breed available in small number in pockets of Bikaner district. The **Marwari** and **Jaiselmeri** are rugged and hardy breeds which can resist severe droughts and travel long distances on migration. The Nali breed produces heavy fleece and is well adopted in the canal area of Ganganagar district.

The sheep of arid region either migrate to nearby places and come back to their native place during rainy season or remain migrated to outside areas throughout the year. Thus two types of migration have been reported.

The flocks in Jodhpur, Pali, Jalore, Sirohi and Ajmer district are generally of Marwari breed. These remain permanently migrated to other districts of South Rajasthan, Madhya Pradesh and Uttar Pradesh. The flocks graze in the forest area of Tonk and Swaimadhopur districts and spend their winter. They keep on moving to forest areas of Bundi and Kota districts. Thereafter these flocks crossover to Madhya Pradesh and keep on moving to Rajgarh and Shivapuri. When summer sets in, the flocks move to Agra and

Mathura Districts in Uttar Pradesh and graze on the harvested fields. With the onset of Monsoon the flocks crossover to Rajasthan and travel back to forest areas of Rajasthan via Bharatpur, Jaipur and Ajmer. These flocks never come back to their native places.

Some of the sheep flocks of arid area also go for temporary migration to the nearby area. The migration entirely depends on the intensity of the monsoon in a particular year. With good monsoon when the pasture conditions are good the migration rate slows down, however, during the drought or scarcity period when the availability of grazing resource and top feeds are poor, the migration rate increases. The migration generally takes place with the onset of winter and is completed with onset of monsoon. The breedwise details of migration are summarised below :

Chokla

Migrates from its natural habitat to the adjoining areas of Haryana in the month of Feb-March. The flock return back to their native place in July.

Nali

These flocks migrate to harvested fields within the district of Ganganagar or at the most in adjoining areas of Punjab and Haryana.

Magra/Pugal

These flocks migrate to **Nali** area of Ganganagar district in Feb-March to graze in harvested fields and return back to their home tract with the onset of monsoon. Purely temporary migration of **Pugal** takes place to Nokha and **Kolayat** areas.

Marwari

The temporary migration of this breed follows the same pattern as in permanent migration except that during monsoon season the flocks spend their time in their home tract.[6]

Table — 41: Sheep Breed of Arid Zone

	Breed	Distribution	Qualitative Characters
1.	Chokla	Churu, Jhunjhunu and Sikar Districts and Common boundries of Bikaner, Jaipur Jodhpur and Nagaur.	Dar Tan face light built, medium Tail and ears
2.	Magra	All over Bikaner alongwith borders of Jaisalmer and Nagaur	Light brown ring around eyes medium built. Long tail, medium ears
3.	Pugal	Pugal area in Western Bikaner district extending upto Pakistan Border	Black face, Light spots around eye medium tail, short ear
4.	Nali	North and North eastern part of Bikaner and whole of Gangangar District	Light brown face. Long ear short tail
5.	Jaisalmeri	North Western part of Jodhpur and Jaisalmer District	Black faced, Long ear and tail light built
6.	Marwari	Jodhpur division, Jaisalmer and Barmer district adjoining area of Ajmer district.	Black faced stocky medium built, short medium tail

Features of Migration

Due to inhospitable climatic conditions and recurrring famine, the Pastoralists of the Western Rajasthan have been put to great hardships. Famines of different kinds, namely, **'akal'** (grain fine), **'jalkal'** (searcity of water), **'tinkal'** (scarcity of fodder), and **'trikal'** (scarcity of fodder, water, and grain) have been of common occurence in this region. This coupled with the degradation and shrinkage of existing pastures, impoverishment of soil conditions and rise in the human population, have forced these sheep farmers to leave their home land in the search of fodder and water. Initially this movement was limited to the adjoining areas. But gradually, with the increase in the means of communication, these sheep farmers learnt much about the availability of grazing lands in the adjoining areas, the routes to be adopted, availability of watering facility, etc. This coupled with the availability of ready market for the products e.g., wool, mutton, milk, manure, etc., encouraged the sheep farmers to extend the dimensions of their migration with sheep and other associated animals. All these factors, therefore, gave rise to nomadic habits amongst the pastoralists.

Large scale migration of sheep farmers alongwith their sheep, goat, camels, and other animals has become one of the prominent features of sheep management in the dry regions of Western Rajasthan. Failure of rains once in every three years is common and occasionally very severe droughts occur at an interval of 15 to 10 years in Rajasthan. During the droughts the land becomes absolutely devoid of vegetation. Owing to such conditions the sheep farmers resort to short and long range migrations. Even otherwise during the hot dry seasons when there is little or no vegetation over left, sheep farmers have to migrate. The migration is sometimes in all directions of the State, depending on easy approach, good rains and availability of pastures. Sometimes it is as far as Bihar in the East, Gujarat in the South-West, Punjab in the North and Madhya Pradesh and Maharashtra in the South. Usually they start migrating after celebrating **Dipavali** and they reach their destination by the month of February and March.

The entire nomadic operations of the pastoral nomads may be understood under the rubric of the following two organizational structures.

DOMESTIC UNIT :

The nomads count their numbers and describe their migratory camp groups in terms of the horde which is locally known as **'DUNG'**. Each such **'Dung'** is occupied by an independent household, typically consisting of an elementary family, and these households, locally called as **'EWAR'** are the basic units of the migratory shepherds'. horde. They are units of production and consumption; represented by their male head who holds right over all the movable property including flocks; and he can even on occasion act as independent units for political purposes.

The external sign of the existence of such a social and nomadic unit is the camp. The camp of the migratory group is always kept half to one mile from the village or town-en-route. The farmers always camp in the open fields without pitching any tent or making any temporary shelter. All the sheep flocks and other animals are folded after the sunset in the centre of the camp. The owner of the flocks keep their belongings at different spots at a distance of about 5 to 80 feet, forming a circle round the folded sheep to ensure safety of the livestock. If, however, in any certain herding unit, the household(ewar) is peopled by only male members, then that particular household is not allowed to dislodge his belongings amidst those herding households which are having housewives and other female members. Although he enjoys all rights of being the members of the horde (dung), but he remains as an outcaste and hence keeps his belonging at least 60 feet away from the main horde. At some places mostly in irrigated tracts of Uttar Pradesh, sheep are folded in the fields at the requests of the agriculturists. In lieu of manuring the field, the sheep farmers get some jaggery,articles of food and sometimes a little cash. Each shepherd acts as a watchman at night, by turn, to check the theft of their sheep or belongings. As a precaution against detection by thieves or cattle lifters the nomads light no fire in the night.

The structure of a herding unit is the home of small family group. In six camp groups of 34 households (Ewar), the average number of persons per 'Ewar' was 5.97 . The household is built around one elementary or joint family of a man, his wife and their children or husband, wife, their married sons,daughters-in-law, and grandchildren. These migrating families are ocasionally supplemented by the addition of unmarried or widowed close relatives, in-laws, and grazier servants (Gwala) who would otherwise be along in their **'Ewar'**. The different types of household in six migratoary camps of the nomads, which were studied, are shown in Table - 42.

Table — 42: Family Type in the Migratory Camp

Type		No.
Incomplete Families		3
Elementary Families		9
Joint Families		8
Composite Families		14
	Total	34

Entire families of the nomads do not move out from their permanent villages; some members are left behind to look after their belongings, cultivation of the meagre land holdings, and to look after the old and feeble members of the family.

The migrating household is a commensal and property - owning group. Though title to animals and some other valuable items of movable property may be vested in individual members of the household, the right to dispose of such is controlled by the head of the household.

The sheep farmers carry a few articles of necessity like a few utensils, blankets, trauplin and ration to maintain individual households. Their ration consists of wheat or **bajra** flour, spices, pulses of gram and **moong.** They pack these articles into the bags made of either camel or goat hair. These packages are loaded on camel, horse, or donkey's back. They also carry some cash to meet the petty expenditure and purchase of a few ration on the way.

A migrating group of shepherds consists of four to fourteen [illegible]s of sheep with a few goats, 6 to 25 camels, 1 to 5 dogs, and 2 to [illegible]eys. Every sheep owner has his distinctive sheep-mark, which [illegible]nbination of a brand **(chokha)** on the sheep's face, back, tail, [illegible]hing or cutting of one ear or both endeavours to be unique. [illegible]e herds may be large, adults have a remarkable ability to [illegible] individual animals; and the sheep - marks are used more [illegible] of the identity of lost sheep vis-a-vis outsiders than to [illegible]uish the animals of different owners who camp together.

[illegible]estic Organization

Within each 'Ewar' (herding unit) there is a distribution of authority and considerable division of labour among the members of the household. But this follows a highly elastic pattern, and it is characteristic that few features of this organization are socially imperative and common to all, while many features vary, and appear to reflect the composition of each household and the working capacities of its members.

All **'Ewars'** have a recognized head, who represents th[illegible] household in dealing with the villagers and other strangers. Wh[illegible] the household contains an elementary family, the hea[illegible] universally the husband in that family, even when widowed fa[illegible] brother resides with the family. Where the 'Ewar' is occupied by an incomplete family, the senior male is the head. Only where there are no adult male members of the household, or where they are temporarily absent, is a woman ever regarded as the head of a household; and in such cases she is usually represented for formal purposes by a close relative.

However, with respect to decisions in the domestic and familiar domain, men and women are more nearly equal, and the distirbution of authority between spouses is a matter of individual adaptation. Thus decisions regarding the multitude of choices in the field of production and consumption (but not decisions about migration routes and camp sites), all matters of Kinship bondings, and decisions that will greatly affect the family, such as whether to change one's group membership, or become sedentary. These are all decisions that are shared by the spouses and to some extent by the other adult members of the household, and in which the wiser or more assertive person dominates, regardless of sex.

Labour is divided among households members by age and sex, but few tasks are rigidly alloted to one sex or one age group. The various labour tasks may be grouped in three categories: **d work, the daily cycle of migration, and tending and he animals.**

Domestic tasks are mainly done by the women and prepare food, wash and mend clothes, bring firewoods water. Spinnng of wool and goat and camel hair is done men and women. Here again there is a strict division of While the women spin only sheep's wool, the men spin on and camel hair (Jatt). The men spin the goat and camel's hair hand spindle (DERHA) and the women spin the wool on **'Charkha'.**

During migration the total distance of about 2000 Kms. is covered in one year at the rate of 8 to 10 kms. a day. About eight months are spent in migration from November to June. Normally, there are about 150 halts of each group of sheep farmers during migration. The halts are mostly of one day at each place and it extends to two to four days in some cases. These frequent migrations of nomads consume much time and labour and strongly ct the organization of the daily round. Activity starts well before daylight, when the sheep and goats, which have spent night by the camp (dung), depart in the care of a shephered who is usually a boy or a man. The camp is usally dismantled around 10 to 11 a.m., when the camels, which are herded separately, return to the camp after grazing the tree leaves. By this time the shepherds entrusted with the duty of herding the sheep and goats generally remain 3 to 5 kms. away from the main camp, and thus, only the head of the household and female members of the **'Ewar'** are left in the camp. When the camels are brought back after the morning grazing, preparations are made to pack and load the household belongings. Packing and loading are done by all, usually in the habitual way but with no formal division of labour. The total process of breaking camp may take about 1 to 1 1/2 hours.

The infants, during migration, are tied on the camel back while the men and women move on foot shepherding their beasts. Usually after two hours travel at a brisk pace, the shepherds determine the route and decide on the place to camp. Camp sites are seized by the individual **'Ewars'** or herding units and the camel caravan dispersed to these sites. All household members co-operate in unloading the beasts. The camels are then let loose and driven off by a child or several children, while the female members are sent off for fetching water from the nearest well and bringing firewood.

The sheep and goats arrive in camp at about noon; after these are milked women prepare a meal. Various domestic tasks are performed in the afternoon; just before sunset the flock is milked again, and the evening meal is taken late, just before going to sleep.

The work of tending the animals consists mainly of herding and milking. The shepherd for the main flock is almost always a male; as he is occupied with the flock from 4 am. to 6 pm. He cannot simultaneously serve as the head of household and perform the male domestic tasks in the tent during migration. Boys down to the age of 6 are therefore frequently used as shepherds, while the elderly and married men only exceptionally do such work. The smaller land less wide-ranging flocks of lambs and kids are usually looked after by smaller children of both sexes; or they may be divided, the weaned ones accompanying the main herd, the unweaned ones tethered in the **'Ewar'**.

Some flock owners, in the event of having insufficient male members for grazing the flocks, employ servants who are known as **'Gwala'**. A **'Gwala'** can either be a **'Raika'** or may belong to other pastoral castes such as the **'Jaat'**, the **'Gujar** and the **'Mohamaden'**. Sometimes a **'Gwala'** is also hired from the lower castes like **'Naik'**. A Raika 'Gwala' may or may not be a distant relative of the Raika flockowner. In the study of 34 Raika flockowner it was discovered that 7 **'Gwalas'** belonged to the **Raika** caste, and out of the 7 Raikas only one **Raika Gwala** was found to be related to his master. Besides the **Raika Gwala,** there were 3 **Jaat, 1 Gujar, 1 Naik,** and one 1 **Natt Gwala** were employed by altogether 11 flockowners. The **'Gwalas'** are generally of age-group between 13 yrs. to 40 years and reside at the distances ranging from the 5 to 30 kms. from the villages of their employer.

The relationship between a shepherd or servant **(gwala)** and his master is based on an explicity economic contract, whereby the former is supplied with food and shelter, new clothes and a pair of shoes, and a salary ranging from Rs. 5000 to Rs.12,000/- per annum; dependng on the age, experience, and incumbents. Such contracts are taken only by propertyless, usually unmarried men, only rarely is the relationship so stable and remunerative for the servant that he can establish a family of his own in the camp.

The partners in such contracts are rarely close kin; on the other hand there is considerable reluctance to engage a shepherd or servant who is an outsider, and even when he is a stranger, since it is necessary to place considerable trust in him, both with regard to his treatment of the animals,and his respect for the family and property of his master. He lives as a member of the household by which he is engaged, but generally eats separate from, or subsequent to , his master.

In a camp it usually happens that the households migrating from one village, keep their 'Ewar' close to each other than those hailing from other villages. This arrangement of households amongst the migrating shepherds can be easily discerned by noting the relative distances between the different **'Ewars'**.

The relationship among members of a herding unit is contractual, and is always regarded as a partnership among equals. Household heads are free to establish the relation with anyone they wish inside their own people. The division of labour between members is based on expediency and the person who serve as shepherd or **'Gwala'** are in no way regarded as the servants of the others, rather, the work they do is regarded as a favour, and rewarded by gifts of lambs. At any time, a member of a herding unit may be withdrawn from that group and work alone, or join another unit; and through time the constellations of households in herding units may change completely.

In order to keep themselves informed about the welfare of the household members in the village, the migrating shepherds keepreleasing one person from every household, turn by turn, to go home and bring the welfare news. While returning from the village, the shepherds also visit the villages of those persons or shepherds who are herding together in one camp and thus convey their welfare. The migrating shepherds also keep remitting letters, written by some literate person of the camp, to inform about their present and future whereabouts.

II. CAMPS

The migratory camps are in some sense the primary communities of the nomadic Society; they correspond to hamlets or small compact villages among sedentary peoples. The members of a camp **(dung)** make up a very clearly bounded social group; their relations to each other as continuing partners are relatively constant, while all other contacts are passing ephemeral, and governed by chance. In what follows I shall attempt to describe the composition of such camp group among the **Raikas,** and analyse their internal structure and organization.

A camp community of nomads can only persist through continuous re-affirmation by all its members. Every day the members of the camp must agree in their decision on the vital question of whether to move on, or to stay camped, and if they move, by which route and how far they should move. These decisions are the very stuff of a pastoral nomad existence; they spell the difference between growth and prosperity of the herd, or loss and poverty. Every household head has an opinion, and the prosperity of his household is dependant on the wisdom of his decision. The maintenance of a camp as a social unit thus requires the daily unanimous agreement by all members on economically vital questions.

Such agreement may be achieved in various ways, ranging from coercion by a powerful leader to mutual consent through compromise by all concerned. The composition of a camp will thus indirectly be determined by the available means whereby the movement of economically independent households can be controlled and co-ordinated. In a sense, recruitment to a camp group is not a once-and-for-all process dependant on the attainment of agreement within the group. The study reveals that ties of Kinship are the underlying principles behind the composition of a migrating camp and I shall base my analysis on the processes whereby the unity of a camp may be determined.

The task of unifying the members of a camp is simplified by the existence of a recognized leader in every camp, who represents the group for political and administrative purposes. The leader of the camp is known as NUMBERDAR who holds his camp together by exercising authority and/or by his influence in establishing and formulating unanimous agreement within the camp on questions of migration and camp sites. Every year before migration the camp leader or **numberdar** is elected. The elected **numberdar** is vested with the powers of including or rejecting any flock-owner. The **numberdar** is elected for a term of one year's camp. The selection of **numberdar** is made out of the elderly persons having sufficient experience of the migratory routes and watering sources. The elected numberdar is expected to discharge his duties faithfully and honestly. Though the **numberdar** is virtually the head of the party but usually he is not burdended with the responsibility of monetary matters.

The normal duties of a **numberdar** are as under:

(i) Searching the pasture lands by conducting short and long distance surveys.

(ii) Allotment of duties to shepherds for grazing sheep, goats, and camels in different directions.

(iii) Making arrangement for location of next camp.

(iv) Contacting the wool merchants, and sheep merchants for the sale of wool and mutton.

(v) Contacting the professional wool shearers and deciding the shearing rate and time and place of wool shearing.

(vi) contacting the agriculturists for getting a cash or kind for folding the sheep in their fields.

(vii) Establishing contacts from the homes of migrating units, sending sheep farmers, turn by turn to homes, sending sheep farmers, turn by turn to homes, and arranging their departure and arrival by rail or road.

(viii) Attending meetings of the Numberdars.

(ix) Settling disputes of sheep farmers trace-passing and theft of animals, etc.

From these duties of the **numberdar** it is quite evident that he is the head of a very well Knit and centralized political system, and has immense authority over all members of the nomads' camp. However, the system does not depend on any delegation of power from the head to subordinates. The office of the headman is usually inherited in male line, with some regard for seniority and experience. However, the members of a camp may insist on their right to appoint anyone as the successor. The authority required for this activity is derived from sources within the camp, and the composition of persisting camp reflects these sources. They are agnatic Kinship in a ramifying descent system, and matrilineal and affinal relations. In the case of an established leader the personal esteem which occures to him for his experience and expediency centres round the network of his kinship relationlships with the members of the camp.

For a camp to persist as a social group, its component herding units must be knit together by the bonds of **agnatic**, **matrilineal**, and particularly **affinal**. Where such bonds are lacking, there are no other structural ties to hold camp group larger than the herding units together, and the devisive effect of the daily decision-making with regard to migration and camping will inevitably lead to fission into multiple migrating units.

The heads of households are interested for their own part in maintaining the bonds that counteract the divisive tendencies. In an established migrating camp, a man's weight in determining policy, and thus in making the daily decisions that control his and his family's life, is dependant on the extent of his influence over other members of his camp. Therefore men prefer to remain within agnatic and matrilineal kin, and seek to establish as many strategically placed affinal bonds within the camp as possible. The same is even more important for the camp leader, who desires both to exert maximal influence within the camp, and to hold it together as a group.

The result is a high frequency of relatives within the camp, implying a high degree of close-knit kinship unity. The genealogical analysis of six migratory camp of the **Raika** nomadic shepherds gives the following frequency of relation between the members of 39 herding units.

(1)	AGNATIC KINS*	:	18(46.15%)
(2)	MATRILINEAL KINS	:	8(20.51%)
(3)	AFFINAL KINS	:	13(33.33%)
	Total	:	39

*Of the 18 Agnatic Kins, there were 10(55.55%) primary agnatic kins and 8(44.44) secondary agnatic kins respectively.

One may, thus, from the preceeding discussions discern three kinds of bonds which have the effect of tying households together in a migratory camp: those of partilineal, and affinal kinship. In addition, occasional service contracts may incorporate shepherds and servants, and their dependents, into camps where they have no ties of Kinship, though distant kins are preferred for such purposes. Finally, a camp's composition may be affected by structurally unpredictable factors such as personal friendships, or the request by refugees from other castes for herding the animals together.

It should be noted that the kinds of claims, the right and duties expected between kinsmen within a camp, are the same whether the relative is a patrilateral or matrilateral collateral, or an affine. Such a system becomes apparent from the patterns of spontaneous and routinized co-operation during migration and in the camp, and in the association and relations of comradeship and respect between kinsmen in general.

PATTERNS OF MIGRATION

Broadly the patterns of nomadic shepherds' migration may be classified as under:

1. Based on Duration

(a) Permanent Migration
(b) Migration For 6 to 9 Months
(c) Migration For 3 to 4 Months
(d) Migration For Short Duration

2. Based On Distance

(i) Migration For Long Distance
(ii) Migration For Short Distance

3. Regular Migration

Before discussing the patterns of nomadic migration under the following heads, it is quite imperative to mention here that unlike the most nomadic communities, the pastoral nomads of Rajasthan have their permanent villages in the districts of Jodhpur,Nagaur, Pali, Barmer, etc. of Western Rajasthan.

1. Based on Duration

(a) **Permanent Migration**: Under permanent migration the sheep flock are not brought to the home village of the sheep farmer at any time. The flockowners however visit their native places at regular intervals. During the Year 1989-90, (see Annexure - I), 12 lakh sheep were on permanent migration. Permanent migratory sheep are mainly grazed in Rajasthan, Madhya Pradesh, and Uttar Pradesh States following definite routes and period as under:—

(i) July to November

Sheep are grazed in the **Dang** (forest) area of Karoli, Sawai - Madhopur, Dholpur, Kota, Bundi, Baran, Jhalawar, Bijolia and Chittorgarh in Rajasthan. During this period some flocks are also grazed in the Shivpuri area of Madhya Pradesh.

(ii) December to February:

During this period sheep are grazed in the **Dang** or forest area of Gwalior, Guna, Shivpuri, Ashoknagar, Rajgarh, Bhelcha, Ujjain, Bhopal, etc. in Madhya Pradesh.

(iii) **March to June**:

During this period sheep are grazed in the areas of Jhansi, Etawh, Dibiyapur, Bala, Kanpur, Chobepur, Mainpuri, Aligarh, Shikohabad, Agra, etc. in Uttar Pradesh. Some flocks are also grazed in Ashoknagar, Bhopal, Indore, and Berar area of Madhya Pradesh.

(b) **Seasonal Migration for 6 to 9 months**: About 20.79 lakh sheep were on seasonal migration during the year 1989-90 from Western and North Western Rajasthan towards Uttar Pradesh, Madhya Pradesh, Delhi, Haryana, Punjab and Gujarat. The sheep farmers migrate to these regions in the month of October and get back to their home village sometime in July. During migration the sheep farmers follow the definite routes (Fig.15) and periods which are as under :–

(i) **Migration to Nagda Area in Madhya Pradesh.**

About 4 lakh sheep migtrate every year from Pali, Jalor and Sirohi districts through the valley of Phulad, Kot, Deguri and Bijapur for reaching Madhya Pradesh. The routes followed by the different groups of shepherds for going to Nagda area in Madhya Pradesh are given below:

1. Jojawar, Kot, Dewgarh, Amet, Chittorgarh, Neemach,Mandasore, Jawara, Chachord, Nagda, Unhel, Indore, Dhar.
2. Ashore, Takhatgarh, Sanderac, Falna, Desuri, Charbhuga, Bansi, Pratapgarh, Mahdsore, Jasora.
3. Desurri, Charbhuja, Mavli, Udaipur, Banswara, Ratlam, Badanagur, Dhar.
4. Jaitaram, Bar, Asind, Vijainagar, Kekri, Bundi, Kota, Rawatbhata, Susner, Agar, Ujjain, Dewas, Hotpipalia, Dhar.
5. Sirohi, Shivganj, Jalna, Desuri, Charbhuja, Mavli, Bansi, Paratapharh, Mandsore, Jaora.

Almost all migratory sheep flocks reach Jaora area by the end of November and from this area the flocks are moved in the following three directions:

1. Klhachrod/Nagda
2. Agar/Alot
3. Ratlam/Badanagar

The flocks remain in the above areas from December to February and then they are moved, after shearing the wool, towards Dhar, Khandwa, Ujjain, Indore, Dewas, Bhopal etc. and the sheep are grazed in the harvested field of Rabi crops upto May-June. The migration towards Nagda area is a regular feature as the sheep flocks are also migrated in this area even during years of good monsoon and good growth of grasses obtaining in the home villages of shepherds of Pali, Jalore, and Sirohi districts.

(ii) **Migration towards Uttar Pradesh & Haryana.**

About 6 lakhs sheep migrate every year from Nagaur, Pali, Jodhpur, Ajmer, Barmer, and Jaisalmer districts. Sheep migrate every year on the following routes which lead them to the region of Uttar Pradesh and Haryana.

1. Degana, Kishangarh, Dudu, Phagi, Sanganer, Dausa, Bharatpur and then to U.P. in Agra, Mathura and Aligarh districts.

2. Bhilara, Jaitaran, Bar, Kishangarh, Dudu, Newai, Sanganer, Daussa, Bharatpur, Uttar Pradesh. From Dausa, migratory flocks are migrated mainly in two directions:

(a) Daussa, Mahuwa, Bharatpur and then to Uttar Pradesh.

(b) Daussa, Mahuwa, Bundi, Kota, Jhalawar, and then to Uttar Pradesh area.

3. Keri, Duni, Bundi, Kota, Jhalawar, and then to Uttar Pradesh.

4. Kekri, Duni, Tonk, Sawai, Madhopur, Karoli, Dholpur and then to Uttar Pradesh Area.

5. Sheep flocks from Nawa, Didwana, Landu, and Sikar area reach Haryana state via Ajitgarh, Alwar, Rewari, Sohna, Gurgaon, Rohtak. The sheep flocks of Barmer and Jaisalmer districts first

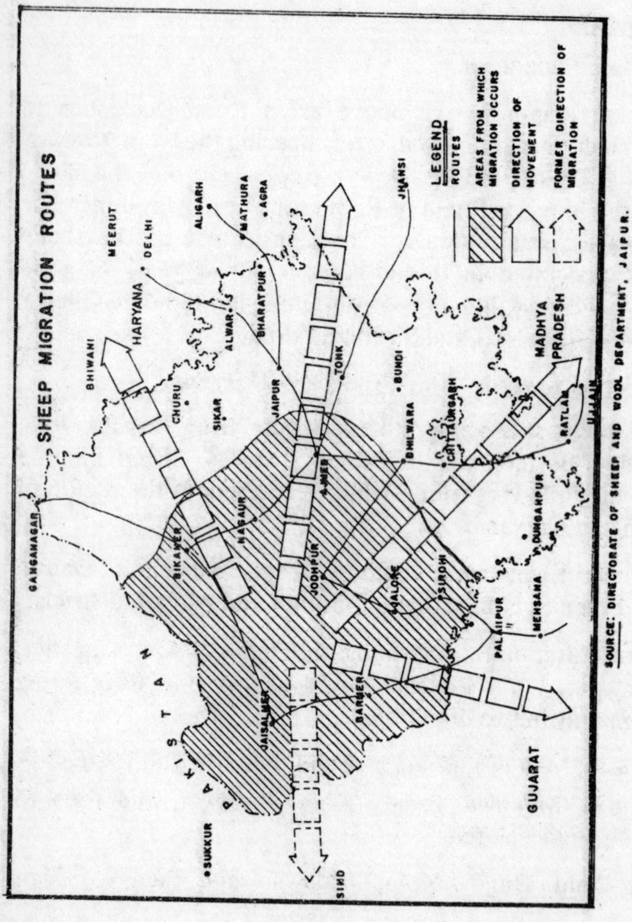

Fig. 15

Source : ORG, Baroda.

reach Banar near Jodhpur, and then they follow the above mentioned routes after reaching Bhilara.

About 70% of migratory flocks remain in Uttar Pradesh and 30% in Haryana during the March - June period. While in Uttar Pradesh, and Haryana, the sheep farmers follow the following routes:

1. Alwar, Gordhan, Mathura, Hathras, Aligarh, Khair.

2. Daussa, Mahua, Bharatpur, Agra, Tundla, Shikohabad, Etawah, Dibiyarpur.

(iii) **Migration towards Gujarat State:-**

About 2 lakhs sheep migrate every year from Sirohi, Jalore, and Barmer districts to Gujarat State. The flocks are moved from home villages during October/November months and grazed in Gujarat State from December to June months, and the flocks are brought back to home village during June/July months. The common migratory routes leading to Gujarat are as follows:

1. Sirohi, Aburoad, Ambaji, Idar, Himatnagar, Shyamlalji, Modasa.

2. Sirohi, Aburoad, Palanpur, Mehsana, Ahmedabad, Baroda.

3. Sumerpur, Sirohi, Ambaji, Idar, Himatnagar, Shyamlalji (some flokcs reach Banswara from Shyamlalji via Dungarpur.)

4. Ahore, Aburoad, Ambaji, Idar, Himatnagar, Modasa.

5. Jalor, Bhimal, Raniwara, Tharad, Dessa, Palanpur.

6. Barmer, Bakasar, Raniwara, Sanhore, Tharad, Deesa, Mehsana, Ahmedabad.

(c) **Migration for 3 to 4 months:**

About two lakhs of sheep from Nokha, Kolayat, Jamsar, Doongarh, Mahajan, Chhapar, Ratangarh, Sardarsahar and Churu areas migrate every year during March and are grazed in Rajasthan canal area from April to June and the flocks are brought back to home villages by the end of June depending upon the monsoon rains.

(d) **Migration for Short Duration:**

In Jodhhpur and Bikaner divisions migration from district to district or within the district for short duration of about 40 to 60 days is quite common. The movement depends upon the availability of good grazing due to adequate rains in a particular area.

2. Based On Distance

(i) Under permanent migration and migration ranging from 6 to 9 months, the sheep flocks cover the long distance of about 2000 kms. in search of good grazing areas.

The sheep farmers make elaborate arrangements for migration on long distances about the selection of **Numberdar,** selection of the relatives and friends, flocks in a group, hired labour (Gwala), camels for transportation, etc. The Raika shepherds while going on migration assimilate the flocks of their relatives and friends residing in the same village.

(ii) **Migration for Short Distance:**

The migration for short distance is resorted to after shearing of the sheep and lambing period in the event of in the absence of grazing facilities in home villages. The migration for short distance is from 20 to 100 km. from home village.

3. Regular Migration

Under regular migration the sheep flocks are migrated every year during definite periods and follow definite routes as continuous process. The main cause of this regular migration is that good grazing areas are available in Uttar Pradesh, Madhya Pradesh, Haryana, and Gujarat State from December to June.

Migration Routes

As per the latest census of 1988 the sheep populaton is 99.13 lakhs. It is estimated that around **15 to 20 lakh sheep migrate and return back** to their home villages with the onset of monsoon rains. The migration usully starts in the month of Oct- Nov. every year, and the flocks return back by the end of June and July months.It may be reiterated that migration is of two types - Temporary and Permanent. In the temporary set up, the flocks return back to their home villages while in the permanent set up the sheep breeders remain in the neighbouring districts of M.P., U.P. and Gujarat forest areas. These permanent migratory sheep flocks come to their home state during the months of July to Oct. so as to avoid heavy rain fall period in these States and save their stock from foot rot infection leading to debility etc. During these 3 to 4 months they remain on the rocky mountain/hilly forest areas of Rajasthan (remain scattered in nine forest districts). These districts are Sawaimadhopur, Bhilwara, Kota, Bundi, Jhalawar, Alwar, Chittor, Bharatpur and Udaipur. It is estimated that these permanent migratory sheep flocks number around 8 to 10 lakhs, depending upon the severity of drought in the State. Later the flocks again move to the forest areas of neighbouring States.

The following information is given about the important routes of migration of the shepherds who move with their sheep flocks and pack animals which never return to the native village of the block owners.

Migratory Routes of Shepherds who Resort to Migration for 6 to 9 months

Sheep migration for 6 to 9 months is a regular practise from the districts of Jaisalmer, Barmer, Jodhpur, Pali, Jalore, Sirohi and Nagaur. The flockowners migrate their sheep from these areas after celebrating **Dipawali** festival in the month of November. Before migration the flocks from each village are grouped together so as to form a large flock comprising 2000 to 5000 sheep. The group of flocks is headed by an experienced and intelligent shepherd of the village who is called **Numberdar**. Such flocks in addition to sheep have a few goats, camels, donkies and dogs. Donkies and camels carry household articles, utensils etc. of the persons going on migration. Women folk from Raikas, Jats, Gujars, and Mohammedans of the village also join in this migration and this composite unit is called 'Dera'.

Largest number of sheep flocks migrate from Merta and Degana Tehsils after celebrating **Dipawali**. Migration of these flocks towards Uttar Pradesh and Haryana takes place by the route (1) Merta, Degana, Parbatsar, Kishangarh, Dudu, Mehlan, Sanganer, Goner, Dausa. (2) Merta, Degana, Nawa, Naraina (From Naraina either to Thanagazi via Gudha, Pratapgarh or Mehlan, Sanganer, Goner, Dausa). Flocks reaching Dausa migrate towards

Migratory Routes of Shepherds whose sheep flocks do not return to the native village

Migratory Routes			Months of Migration
Starting Place (Dist.)	Moving Through	Going up-to (Dist./State)	
1	2	3	4
Jalore	Sirohi, Ratlam	Nagda (MP)	Nov. - July
Jodhpur	Pali, Falan, Neemach, Ratlam	Nagda (MP)	-do-
Jodhpur	Ajmer, Sawai-Madhopur, Bundi, Jhalawar, Ujjain, Indore		November
Jaisalmer	Barmer, Jodhpur and Jalore via Sanchore, Tharad, Deesa and Palanpur	Agra (U.P)	Nov. Dec.
Ajmer	Niwai, Chaksu, Lalsot, Dholpur, Agra	Agra (U.P)	Nov. Dec.
Jalore Pali and Nagaur	Ajmer, Jaipur Chaksu, Dholpur, Lalsolt, Gangapur, Gwalior, Bhind, Itawa, Mainpuri	Mainpur (U.P)	Nov. July
Ajmer	Niwai, Sawai, Madhopur, Shivpuri, Konch, Orai, Dibiapur	Dibiapur (U.P)	Nov. July
Ajmer	Jaipur, Dausu, Bharatpur, Agra, Hathrus, Aligarh	Aligarh (U.P)	Jan. February and March.

Uttar Pradesh via Mahuwa, Bharatpur and those reaching Thanagazi migrate towards Haryana. Some flocks from Jodhpur and Pali districts reach Dudu via Bilara, Jaitaran, Bar, Kishangarh or Bilara, Jaitaran, Pisangan, Kishangarh, Dudu. From Dudu these flocks move towards Uttar Pradesh or Haryana via Dausa or Thanagazi.

Flocks migrating towards Madhya Pradesh from Nagaur, Pali and Ajmer districts first reach Kekri and then to Dooni; from Dooni either towards Bundi, Kota, Jhalawar, Kkelera, Rajgarh, Byawara or from Dooni to Tonk, Sawai Madhopur, Karauli, Dholpur and then to Uttar Pradesh. A few flocks from Jalore district migrate to Haryana or Uttar Pradesh. The routes being Ahore, Bhadrajun, Pali, Sojat, Bar, Kekri, Dooni, Tonk, Niwai, Chaksu, Lalsot, Dausa. From Dausa these move either towards Thanagazi and Alwar to Haryana or towards Uttar Pradesh via Dausa, Mahuwa and Bharatpur.

About 1 to 2 lac sheep from Jaisalmer, Barmer, Jodhpur and Jalore areas also migrate to Gujrat State via Sanchore, Tharad, Deesa, Himatnagar and Palanpur.

A few old and diseased stock is left back in the villages and few persons remain backhome to lookafter their land and other livestock.

Except the flocks of Barmer and Jaisalmer districts the flocks of remaining districts migrate towards south in Madhya Pradesh. Migration of these flocks towards south takes place through various routes, one is Jalore, Sirohi, Ratlam, Nagda, Second being Jodhpur, Pali, Falna, Neemach, Ratlam, Nagda and the third being Jodhpur, Ajmer, Sawai-Madhopur, Bundi, Kota, Jhalawar, Ujjain, Indore and Nagda. From Ajmer a few flocks migrate via, Bhilwara, Chittorgarh and Nagda.

Thus Nagda in Madhya Pradesh is the central place where sheep are booked for wool sale. The flockowners are having this regular feature of wool transactions at Nagda for the last 40 years. A large number of shearing takes place within a radius of 15-20 k.m from Nagda but a few flocks are also shorn as long a distance as Ujjain, Indore, Dewas, and Khandwa, some flocks are also shorn at Shivpuri and Bhopal areas. The sheep in this area are shorn in greasy form during months of December to January.

Some of the flocks from Jaisalmer and Barmer migrate only upto Jodhpur, Nagaur, Jaipur areas, but during very acute conditions these flocks proceed towards Agra via Bharatpur and Alwar.

Sheep flocks comprising about 1 lac from Bikaner, Churu, Sikar districts usually migrate towards north in the areas of Punjab, Haryana and Delhi.

About three lac sheep from the districts of Nagaur, parts of Jodhpur, Pali, Jalore migrate towards east in Uttar Pradesh. These flocks follow the belts of Chambal and Jamuna rivers. The migratory routes are Ajmer, Jaipur, Chaksu, Lalsot, Gangapur, Dholpur, Morena, Gwalior, Bhind and Itawa and another route being Ajmer, Jaipur, Dausa, Bharatpur, Agra, Hathras, Aligarh. These flocks, which migrate towards Uttar Pradesh have three important shearing points-Dibiapur, Itawa, Mainpuri - Agra-Hathras areas. Dibiapur is the Central place of shearing in Uttar Pradesh. Migration in this area is taking place since last 35 years.

All these flocks migrating towards Madhya Pradesh and Uttar Pradesh start their journey back to their homes in Rajasthan by the first week of June and reach their respective villages by the time monsoon rains have set in.

Migratory Routes of Shepherds in Madhya Pradesh

The migratory sheep from Rajasthan enter into the forests and other areas of Madhya Pradesh after crossing Chambal river at Dholpur, Rohdai, Dhebri, Kota, Gandhisagar and Noli-dam.

After entering into Madhya Pradesh State the routes followed by the migratory flocks are mentioned below, which also indicate number of sheep, goat, camel etc. and the period of their stay in that State.

The migratory shehereds stay in the forests of Madhya Pradesh from October to March, and the sheep flocks mainly thrive on grasses, shrubs and leaves of certain species of vegetation.

From the month of March to the start of rainy season these migratory shepherds move towards harvested fields of Madhya Pradesh and Uttar Pradesh. During this period these sheep thrive well on the crop residue of wheat, mustard, gram etc. With the onset of rains, these flocks enter the forest areas of **Karauli, sar-Mathura, Barundhan** forest ranges (Bundi), **Kota, Baran, Jhalawar**

Sl. No.	Migratory Route	Length of Route in M.P	Duration of stay	Quantities of various categoaries of cattles.			
				Sheep	Goat	Camel	Horse
1.	Sawai Madhopur (Raj) Palighat (Chambal river border), Sheopur, Karel, Pohari, Shivpuri, Mohna, Gwalior, Bhind (U.P)	(416km.)	80 to 90 days	60000 (About 20 Dung)	200	400	20
2.	Shahbad (Raj.) Bamori, (M.P. Check-Post), Guna, Ashok Nagar, Isagarh, Chanderi, Lalitur (U.P) Chanderi to Pichhor, Ktera, Datia, Jhansi (U.P.)	(240km.)	50 to 60 days	75000 (About 25 Dung)	250	500	50
3.	Ekera(Raj) Bhojpura (M.P Check-post, Khilchipur Rajgarh, Biawara Satalia, Lateri, Sironj, Vidisha, Raisen, Sagar, Chhatarpur, Jatara, (Checkpost	(496km)	100 to 120	75000 (About 25 Dung)	250	500	50

(*Contd.*)

	distt. Tikamgarh) Mahuranipur (UP) Rohat (U.P). Hamirpur Yamuna Bridge, U.P.)						
4.	Bhawani Mandi (Rajasthan) Dag (Raj.) Susner (M.P.Border) Agara Bin, Devas, Sonkutchh, Harda, Chinchali, Bettul, Achnessar (Checkpest) Amaravati (Maharashtra)	(496km)	100 to 120 days	75000 (About 25 Dung)	250	500	200
5.	Nimbaheda (Rajasthan) Nimach, Mandsour, ZAWRA Khachrod, Nagda, Bednaga, Dhar, Badnawar, Ratnam, Namli, Banswara (Rajasthan)	(384km)	80 to 90 days	45000 (About 15 Dung)	150	300	150
Total			3,30,000 Sheep	1100 Goat	2200 Camel	470 Donkeys Horse.	

and Mandalgarh (Bhilwara districts). Thus the shepherds remain with their flocks in Rajasthan area till the rainy season is over and then enter into Madhya Pradesh forest areas again in the beginning of October.

The migratory sheep from Rajasthan have been regularly permitted into forest areas of Madhya Pradesh for the last nearly 60 years with a valid transit permit issued by the Madhya Pradesh authorities after charging grazing fees. In order to regulate the entry and movement of these migratory sheep into forest areas of Madhya Pradesh, the Government has now imposed certain restrictions from 1978-79. Under these regulations the migratory sheep are permitted with a valid transit permit at only three points from Rajasthan viz. Palighat, Shahbad Bamori and **Eklora-Khilchipur**. The movement in the forest areas has been restricted to only three routes and that too for 45 days only viz. (1) Palighat, Sheopur-Karhal, Pohari-Shivpuri, Mohana, Gwalior, Bhind and then Etawa in Uttar Pradesh. (2) Shahbad-Bamori, Guna, Ishagarh, Chandari, Lakitpur and then in Uttar Pradesh towards Orai. (3) Eklera, Khilchipur, Rajgarh, Chandari and then in Uttar Pradesh towards Orai.

Migration of shepherds for 6 to 9 months also takes place in Madhya Pradesh and the Shepherds start from their homes after celebrating **Dipawali** festival. The number of shepherds migrating for 6 to 9 months to this area is 3 to 4 lacs. The shepherds enter Madhya Pradesh during the months of November-December through Mandsor, Rajgarh and move in the areas of Ratlam, Dhar, Indore, Shajahpur, Bhopal and return to their home villages by the time the rains set in.[7]

RECENT TRENDS IN NOMADIC PASTORALISM

The pattern of nomadic and semi-nomadic pastoralism has been undergoing a change during the last few decades. There are several reasons which account for this trend. In the first place, the extent of area available for grazing has gone down tremendously with the extension of area under cultivation. This increasing and unfavourable ratio of grazing land to livestock has disturbed the balance. Advent of irrigation through Rajasthan canal has also generated a great deal of changes in the nomadic pastoralism. In what follows, an attempt is made to describe the various types of changes that have been taking place in the patterns of nomadic and semi-nomadic pastoralism in arid zone of Rajasthan.

Ancestral Migration Patterns

A study conducted by **Kavoori**[8] revealed that a considerable majority (67%) of the pastoralist families that now migrate told that their grandfather did not practice a migratory way of life. This appeared to have been true of all major pastoral communities who practice migration. Among the major pastoral communities,the **Raika** provide the highest proportion of migrants, with the **Jats** a close second. In the case of **Rajputs** and **Sindhi Muslims**, however, it was found that a rather fewer proportion were migrating in the past. Approximately three fourths from these groups were not migrating earlier. The picture is more or less similar from the point of view of a district-wise distribution of migrating forefather, with Jaisalmer (mainly Rajputs and Sindhi Muslims) alone showing a distinctly lower rate of out migration (See Table - 43 and 44).

Table — 43 : Whether Grandfather Migrated (Castewise)

Caste	Non-Migrate	%	Migrant	%	Total
Raika	56	(62.2)	33	(36.6)	90
Rajput	39	(72.2)	15	(27.7)	54
Jat	44	(66.6)	22	(33.3)	66
Gujar	5	(55)	4	(45)	9
Muslim	29	(82)	6	(18)	34
S.C	4	(45)	5	(55)	9
Others	4	(80)	1	(20)	5

Table — 44 : Whether Grandfather Migrated (Base Districtwise)

District	Non-Migrant	%	Migrant	%	Total
Pali	29	(56.8)	16	(34.7)	46
Nagaur	42	(67.7)	20	(32.2)	62
Jodhpur	33	(62.2)	20	(37.7)	53
Barmer	26	(59.0)	18	(40.9)	44
Jaisalmer	50	(80.6)	12	(19.3)	62

Those forefathers who migrated, it was revealed that the greatest number went to Uttar Pradesh, a considerable number to Madhya Pradesh and Haryana. A few cases of migration into Gujarat were also reported. Regarding the number of years since the forefathers respondents themselves started migrating, it was found that almost a quarter of the sampled respondents commenced migration for the first time in the last two years alone. About 40% of the respondents had migrated for less than five years.These constitute an indication of the increase in the rate of acceleration. The remaining respondents reported a spectrum of five to over twenty years of personal experience of migration.

The enquiry into the patterns of migration between the decade 1977 to 1988 revealed that more than one and half times the number of people did not migrate at the begining of the decade than at its close. Leaving aside 1988, the figure for migrants in 1987 is slightly over twice that in 1977. Even between 1987-88, the magnitude of the jump (from 189 to 268 cases), suggests the widespread nature of exodus in that year (Table 45). The Table 46 presents the details of those that migrated. It is clear from this table that over the ten year period the local migrant population show

Table — 45: 1977 to 1988 : Extent of Migration

	Non-Migration		Migration	
	Cases No.	Proportion %	Cases No.	Proportion %
1988	0	0	268	100
1987	79	29	189	70
1986	98	37	170	63
1985	123	46	145	54
1984	139	52	129	48
1983	155	58	113	42
1982	161	60	107	40
1981	170	64	98	36
1980	175	66	93	34
1979	179	67	89	33
1978	183	69	85	31
1977	181	68	87	32

Table – 46: 1977 - 1988 : Type of Migration

	Local cases	Migration Proportion	Long Rang Cases	Migration Proporation	Intera cases	State Proportion	Inter Cases	State Proportion
	No.	%	No.	%	No.	%	No.	%
1988	11	4	257	95	75	29	182	71
1987	31	16	158	83	53	33	104	66
1986	32	18	137	80	51	37	86	63
1985	28	19	117	80	47	40	70	60
1984	25	19	104	80	40	38	64	62
1983	17	15	96	84	36	37	60	63
1982	18	16	89	83	31	34	58	65
1981	14	14	84	85	26	30	58	69
1980	15	16	78	83	25	32	53	68
1979	15	16	74	83	25	33	49	66
1978	11	12	74	87	25	33	49	66
1977	10	11	76	87	25	32	50	68

limited but steady increase in number unitl 1987-88, when there is a halt followed by total decline, indicating that those who were previously local migrants were forced to out migrate at this juncture. Throughout the entire period however the proportion of local migrants constitute at the most less than one fourth of the total number of migrants. The great majority (over 80%) of the migrant shepherds are therefore committed to long distance and long duration migrations. This group shows a steady increase in numbers from 76 in 1977 to slightly over twice that figure in 1988. The data on migration within and outside Rajasthan indicates that a slightly larger number and proportion of migrants moved out to bordering States.

The data (Table 47) on the distribution of the shepherds who migrated outside Rajasthan indicate the emergence of Haryana as a major area of migration. Excepting Maharashtra, all the States show significant increase in the number of migrants, Gujarat and Haryana however, show higher rates of growth, increasing ten and five-fold respectively. The shepherds moving towards Uttar Pradesh also doubled over the period. In contrast, leaving aside the period 1987-88, the population moving into Madhya Pradesh remains relatively stable through the period, consqeuently the relative share of migrants received by Madhya Pradesh actually declined. 1987-88 sees a very large increase in the number of migrants to Madhya Pradesh and is reflective of the shift in migration pattern that was a feature that year.

Though there has been steady growth in absolute number of the migrant shepherds,from the five arid districts where study was conducted, higher rates of increase in out-migration was found for the three relatively more arid districts. Thus, while **Jaisalmer** district shows a fifteen-fold increase (Table 48), and **Barmer** and **Jodhpur** increase by three times, **Pali** and **Nagaur**, both semi-arid districts, do not show such dramatic increase. Equally significant are the changes in relative share that emerge over this period. At the beginning of the period over 60% of the migrants belonged to Pali and Nagaur districts. At the end of the period this share is down to 40%. In contrast the relative share of Jaisalmer increases from a mere 4.5% of the total to almost a quarter by the end of the period.

Table – 47 :1977-1988, Direction of Migration

Year	Haryana Cases	%	M.P Cases	%	U.P Cases	%	Gujarat Cases	%	Maharashtra Cases	%
1988	93	34.7	42	15.6	22	8.2	23	8.5	2	0.7
1987	46	24.3	18	9.5	25	13.2	12	6.3	2	1.0
1986	38	22.3	20	11.7	16	9.4	11	6.4	1	0.5
1985	32	22.0	12	11.7	15	10.3	6	4.1	0	0
1984	27	20.9	18	13.9	13	10	6	4.6	0	0
1983	26	23.0	13	15.5	14	12.3	6	5.3	1	0.8
1982	21	19.6	14	13	15	14.0	8	7.4	0	0
1981	16	16.3	17	17.3	19	19.3	5	5.1	1	1.0
1980	15	16.1	17	18.2	17	18.2	3	3.2	1	1.0
1979	13	14.6	21	23.5	12	13.4	3	3.0	0	0
1978	16	18.8	18	21.1	13	15.2	2	2.3	0	0
1977	16	18.3	19	21.8	14	16.0	2	2.2	0	0

Table – 48 : 1977 - 1988 Past Migration by Base Districts

Year	Rali Cases	%	Nagaur Cases	%	Jodhpur Cases	%	Barmer Cases	%	Jaisalmer Cases	%
1988	46	17.1	62	23.1	53	19.7	44	16.4	63	23.5
1987	40	21.1	45	23.8	38	20.1	28	14.8	38	20.1
1986	40	23.5	40	23.5	35	20.5	25	14.7	30	17.6
1985	38	26.2	32	22	26	17.9	24	16.55	25	17.2
1984	35	27.1	31	24	24	18.6	20	15.5	20	15.5
1983	31	27.4	26	23	20	17.6	20	17.6	16	11.5
1982	30	28	25	23.3	20	18.6	18	16.8	14	13
1981	30	30.6	24	24.4	19	19.3	15	15.3	10	10.2
1980	28	30.1	26	27.9	17	18.2	13	13.9	9	9.6
1979	27	30.3	27	30.3	16	17.9	13	14.6	6	6.7
1978	23	27.0	29	34.1	16	18.8	12	14.1	5	5.8
1977	24	27.5	31	35.6	16	18.3	12	13.2	4	4.5

The Process of Migratory Drift

The south and south-eastern borders of the Rajasthan state are the regions which harbour large tracts of forest lands, and are known to the pastoralists as the **Daang.** Characteristic freature of these tracts include forest cover, irregular topography including ravines and bad- lands, minor hill ranges, rivulets and streams, combined with the relative absence of habitation and cultivation. In the past, pastoral migrations from the western regions of arid Rajasthan to **Malwa** and the **Daang** area have been a regular phenomenon. *Malwa* as its name denotes refers to crop land, and must be clearly distinguished from the **Daang.** The migration were by and large seasonal in natural and involved a movement from the base region to the Daang for the winter and then to Malwa after the harvest, and subsequent return to the regions of the origin.

The last three decades or so have seen the development of a shift away from this pattern to the movement on a more permanent basis into the forested areas which Kavoori[9] refers to as the process of a **migratory drift.** This process involves two developments - one minor shift in the routes of migration and two, an elongation of the cycles of migration. When grazing resources declined significantly in the home districts of the migratory shepherds, they stopped returning every year to their native village with their flocks and instead opted to extend the period of their migration to next year by maintaining a localised cycle of movement between the **Daang** and the harvested fields of **Malwa.** Over a period of time however this became an increasingly frequent practice, especially among owners of the largest flocks whose grazing requirements were the heaviest. Thus a pattern emerged whereby flocks stopped returning to the village bases in the districts of Nagaur, Pali, Jalore in Rajasthan and Kuchch in Gujarat for increasingly longer periods, and **finally** to a situation where they stopped returning altogether. Thus, as per the 1989-90 statistics on sheep migration from Rajasthan State, there were about 1.20 million sheep who were on permanent migration. Their owners continue to maintain strong links with their villages of origin but their flocks never return. In the course of time these flocks have developed their own distinctive patterns of movements, involving shifts from the **Daangs** of Rajasthan and Madhya Pradesh to the arable lands of Madhya Pradesh, and Uttar Pradesh. The flocks thus retained their nomadic character, but in the pattern and context of migration, however, there has been a shift. The extent to which the number of sheep are resorting to permanent migration since the year 1983-84 to 1989-90 may be seen in Annexure - I.

Haryana - New Area for Migration

The rise of an irrigation based agriculture in Haryana state falling on the northern border of Rajasthan, has played a crucial role in the evolution of the present day pattern of nomadic pastoralism. Prior to the advent of irrigation the Haryana state was little more than a continuation of the semi-arid tracts of **shekhawati.** It has only been in the last quarter centrum with the introduction of canal irrigation in the region that the green revolution has transformed the face of its countryside. The significant effect of this agricultural explosion was the creation of a new adaptive niche for the pastoralists the form of crop stubble in a previously barren region of Haryana.

Migration on Trucks

The year 1987 emerged to be significant for the nomadic pastoralists as the severe drought situation, which prevailed in the Western districts of Rajasthan - especially in Jaisalmer, Bikaner, Barmer, Jodhpur Bikaner, and Naguar, led to a series of exceptional developments. The two year successive droughts forced the pastoralists to migrate with their flocks to the neighbouring States in search of fodder. As per the usual practice, they started return journey for their village before monsoon. But when they reached their native villages, they found to their utter dismay that in majority of the western districts, there was no monsoon showers and only a few areas had received little rain. This resulted in accumulation of all the migratory flocks in very few areas for fodder and water where rain had poured. Consequently all the available fodder got exhausted within a month which in a normal year of rainfall lasts up-to October. Thus the month of August, 1987 confronted the flock owners with a grim prospect - the complete exhaustion of all grazing resources.

In the given circumstances, when the single-crop semi-arid tracts of Jodhpur, Naguar and Ajmer could not have provided grazing resources of crop stubbles, the flocks owners decided to adopt a new method. Since the only place where the flocks could graze in this period was the **Daang** of east and south-east of Rajasthan and the adjoining Madhya Pradesh State, the flock owners hired hundred of trucks to transport lakhs of sheep to the area around Kota district, and from there these flocks then marched into the forest belts of **Daang**. This method proved to be successful as the flocks, which could have otherwise perished, managed to pull through up to the winter.[10]

This new trend of transporting the sheep flocks on trucks, which started as a measure to combat drought situation in August 1987, has now a days become a common practice for the nomadic pastoralists especially under the following circumstances:

(i) When there is large number of new-born sheep in the flocks who cannot travel long distances during migration on foot.

(ii) When the shepherds undertake migration to **Daang** and harvested crop fields around February or March after exhausting the locally available fodder. During this period the shepherds resort to migration on trucks since the agriculturists resent their movements through the fields with standing rabi crops.

(iii) When the sheep flocks contain large number of weak and diseased sheep unable to travel long distances on foot.

(iv) When the shepherds fail to get hired graziers (gwala).

(v) When due to some personal problem, the individual shepherds fail to join the other migratory flocks at the time of migration after **Dipawali** festival, and

(vi) When on return journey, the shepherds want to prevent the loss in body weight of the mutton sheep, and to avoid confrontation with the stationery cattle owners over the use of grazing grasses in the districts of Kota, Jhalawar, Bundi, Chittorgarh, etc.

Impact of Irrigation

Advent of irrigation through Rajasthan canal, popularly known as the **Indira Gandhi Nahar Pariyojana (IGNP)** has generated a great deal of changes in its wake. With a view to understanding the impact of the IGNP on the lives of the pastoralists, the Operations Research Group[11] (ORG), Baroda undertook a research study in 1991. The IGNP is a large irrigation project in the desert area of north-west Rajasthan. The main canal is 445 kms long and runs approximately parallel to the international boundary. It includes all the lands between these two lines. The total GCA of project is 17.17 lac ha. and has been divided into two stages for convenience in planning, construction and administrative control. The stage-I command has 189 kms long main canal to serve CCA of 5.25 lac ha.. Most of the construction work has been completed and area is under irrigation since few years. The stage II command has been planned to serve an area of 10.12 lac. ha through 256 km. main canal and 5115 kms of distribution system. The command area lies in the districts of Ganganagar, Churu, Bikaner, Jaisalmer, Barmer and Jodhpur (Fig. 16).

The study revealed that about 73 per cent respondents in stage-I are already settled at one place and practice irrigated agriculture. Families including landless (27 per cent) still maintain large herds and flocks and generally migrate outside the command for a period of 3 to 4 months in a year. However, in stage-II almost all the respondents have expressed their readiness to settle at one place provided adequate irrigation water for their fields is given. The sheep farmers stressed that besides irrigation water, open grazing pasture lands should also be made available for their sheep flocks. Although in stage-I about 73 per cent respondents are practising cultivation along with livestock husbandry, the sizes of the flocks have been reduced and there is a gradual change from sheep and goat to cattle rearing. It was also found through the study that although 61 per cent respondents still resort to seasonal migration, in stage II, only 6 per cent respondents opined that they would continue to migrate with their flocks even after getting irrigation facility for their agricultural fields. One interesting aspect of the irrigation development in the desert regions has been that the pastoralists, who were landless and failed to get land from the government and used to manage the fodder requirements for their flocks from the fallow lands and locally available pastures, have now started going on migration with the flocks as the pasture lands have now been brought under double-cropping cultivation due to availability of irrigation water through the Indira Gandhi Canal.

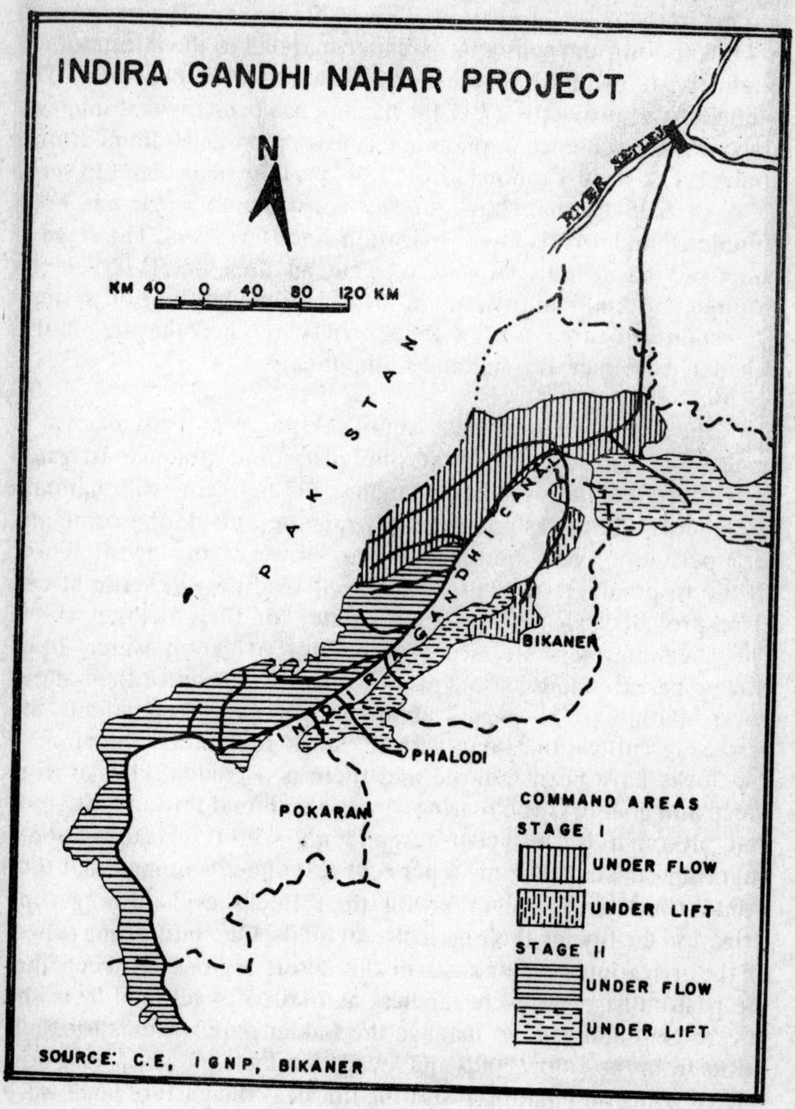

Fig. : 1 6
Source : ORG, Baroda.

Theka System

Stubble grazing in the crop harvested fields has traditionally been one of the important sources of providing feed to the sheep during migration. About 20 years back, the farmers were allowing the flockowners to graze the migratory sheep flock in the harvested fields without taking any money. Instead, the farmers gave some cash money and food grains to the flockowners in lieu of folding the sheep in the agricultural fields and thus receving very good natural manure in the form of animal droppings. But things have changed now.The owners of the crop harvested fields are now demanding money from the migratory flockowners for allowing their sheep and goat to graze in the fields. Although this practise is not uniform in all the States through which the migratory shepherds travel, this practise was found to be quite common in Gujarat state and Konch tahsil (sub-divison) of Jalun distriact in Uttar Pradesh State. Over the years this practise has been formalised and is known as **'Theka'** system. **Theka** means contract. Under this system, the owners of the crop harvested fields enter into a contract through the **Sarpanch** (president of the village Panchayat (Council). It is decided that the flock owners would pay money to the **Sarpanch** for utilizing the grazing land. The amount is decided on the basis of the area of the grazing land and duration for which the flocks would graze in the contracted fields. The amount thus collected by the **Sarpanch** is spent on the welfare of the village community and improving the infrastructure facilities in the village like providing drainage system, repairing school buildings, repairing or laying new roads, maintenance of temples, etc. The main advantage of this **Theka** system is that it eliminates scopes for any conflict between the flock owners and the land owners. The flockowners are also happy with this system as money they spend in securing the contract is recovered to a great extent in the form of the cash and kind gifts which they receive from the individual land owners in lieu of the animal droppings.

REFERENCE

1. Singh, V.K. 1991. Migration of Sheep In North Western Arid Region of Rajasthan. **Paper Presented at Natonal Workshop on Sheep Migration at Jaipur,** 6 - 7 February, 1991.

2. **Interim Report of the National Commission On Agriculture on Poultry, Sheep and Pig Production, Government of India,** New Delhi, 1973.

3. Moulik, T.K. and V. Hariharan 1986. Sheep Rearing and Wool Production in India : Problems and Prospects, **IIM., Ahmedabad.**

4. Chowdhary, B. and B. Singh. 1974 Natural Pastures - Grasses and Shrubs for Sheep and other Ruminants in the Western Arid Zone of Rajasthan. **Ext. Bulletin** No. 1. Dept. of Animal Production College of Veterinary and Animal Science, Bikaner, Op. cit Singh, V.K. 1991.

5. Chowdhary, B.R. 1981 Sheep Management practices in rural areas of Rajasthan. **In Status of Sheep in India - 1st proceeding of the Society and National Seminar on Sheep and Goat Production and Utilisation.**

6. Op. cit. Singh, V.K. 1991.

7. **Report on Migration of Sheep, 1979. Government of Rajasthan.**

8. Kavoori, P.S 1990. Pastoral Transfermance in Western Rajasthan : A Report on the Migratory System of Sheep. **Institute of Development Studies, Jaipur** (India).

9. Ibid.

10. Ibid.

11. Report of the Study on Socio-economic Evaluation of Pastoral Families in IGNP Command Operations 1991 Research Group, Baroda.

6

Problems of Pastoral Nomadism

The livestock industry of arid areas in Western India, so dependent upon pastoral exploitation, so important in the subsistence of specialists and subsidiary husbanders alike, is currently undergoing a phase of severe involution, a downward spiral reflected in the declining resources and declining productivity[1].

The human population of Rajasthan increased 33% between 1971 and 1981, and this is a continuation of an ongoing expansion. The desert districts of Barmer, Jodhpur and Jaisalmer increased in population over the last decade 44%, 45% and 45% respectively. A similar pattern is found with the livestock population. In Rajasthan as a whole, the livestock population (mixed species) rose from 34 million in 1957 to almost 50 million in 1983, and there was an increase in livestock density from 99 per sq.km. to 145 per sq.km . In desert districts, where sheep and goats predominate (over 70% of the total), the livestock numbers just about doubled between 1956 to 1983, from 800,000 to 1,500,000 in Jaissalmer, from 1,600,000 to 3,00,000 in Barmer, and from 1,500,000 to 3,500,000 in Jodhpur. As regards landuse, the area sown in Rajasthan as a whole increased from 32% in 1954 to 44% in 1981, as did the protected forest land, up from 4% to 6%, while fallow land decreased from 18% to 19%. In sum, the human population of Rajasthan has increased greatly, and even more so in the desert districts. Concomitantly, the agricultural area sown has increased substantially, as has the protected forest land, and the uncultivated land available for grazing has diminished appreciably. Livestock numbers has increased greatly. The result is much higher livestock density on the land, and a decrease of pasture and water available per animal, and an inevitable decline in the condition of the livestock and a degradation of the pasture[2].

As Bose[3] puts it: the extent of the area available for grazing has gone down tremendously with the extension of area under cultivation. This increasingly unfavourable grazing land to livestock ratio has disturbed the balance and breeders find it difficult to raise large herds. Their earnings have gone down and the quality of their livestock has deteriorated." The statistics for the decade since Bose wrote, and his reference was based upon research done a decade earlier yet, indicate substantial worsening of the grazing land/ livestock ratio and increase of the pressures on the pastoralists.

The availability of grazing lands per unit of livestock in important districts of Rajasthan is shown in Table - 49. The table shows that in almost all arid districts, there was a slow but sure decline in the grazing area per livestock population. According to the estimation of demand and supply of fodder in Rajasthan by

Table 49: Livestock population and Grazing land per unit of Livestock Population in Arid District of Rajasthan.

District	Total grazing ground ('000ha)	Total live-stock popula-tion in (1972) ('000)	Grazing land per unit of live-stock (1972) (Ha)	Total live stock popula-lation in (1983) ('000)	Grazing land per unit of livestock (1983) (Ha)	% Change in pop-ulation (1972-83)
Bikaner	1738	899	1.93	2091	0.83	132.59
Barmer	736	1974	0.37	3248	0.23	64.54
Chur	209	1426	0.15	2043	0.10	43.27
Jodhpur	1088	1893	0.57	2667	0.41	40.89
Jaisalmer	3783	616	6.14	1616	2.34	162.34
Ganganagar	386	1534	0.25	2199	0.18	43.35
Sikar	121	1530	0.08	1761	0.07	15.10
Jhunjhunu	71	979	0.07	1176	0.06	20.12
Nagaur	184	2304	0.08	3028	0.06	31.42
Jalore	149	1235	0.12	1475	0.10	19.43

Animal Husbandry Department of State Government, 20 districts showed a fodder deficiency and only 7 districts showed a surplus availability of fodder as shown in Table 50. This fodder deficiency

Table 50: Demand and Supply of Fodder in Rajasthan

S.No.	Districts	Number of Adult Cattle Units(A.C.U. in lacs)			Total requirement of fodder (lac tonnes)	Total fodder Production in lac tonnes	Gap in lac tonnes
		Cattle + Buffaloe	Sheep	Other live-stock			
1.	Ajmer	5.46	1.61	1.23	16.60	10.41	−6.19
2.	Alwar	6.96	2.70	1.93	23.18	13.26	−9.92
3.	Banswara	5.74	0.05	0.25	12.08	6.43	−5.65
4.	Barmer	4.25	2.28	6.75	26.56	37.47	−10.86
5.	Bharatpur	5.20	0.20	0.67	12.14	8.12	−4.02
6.	Bhilwara	7.85	1.94	1.96	23.50	122.64	−10.86
7.	Bikaner	4.25	2.24	3.00	18.98	19.65	+0.67
8.	Bundi	6.86	0.25	0.92	16.06	7.20	−8.86
9.	Chittorgarh	7.44	0.41	1.30	18.30	11.74	−6.56
10.	Churu	2.97	1.58	5.61	20.32	23.46	+3.14
11.	Dhoplur	2.52	0.03	0.34	5.78	3.07	−2.71
12.	Dungarpur	4.79	0.45	0.67	11.82	3.54	−8.28
13.	Ganganagar	7.87	1.29	5.30	28.92	25.80	−3.12
14.	Jaipur	12.33	1.08	2.96	32.74	32.10	−0.64
15.	Jaisalmer	2.13	1.87	2.80	13.60	13.55	−0.05
16.	Jalore	4.11	1.11	1.65	13.74	14.09	+0.35
17.	Jhalawar	5.40	0.05	0.75	12.40	17.60	+5.20
18.	Jhunjhunu	2.37	0.48	2.49	10.68	10.65	−0.03
19.	Jodhpur	5.17	2.35	3.47	21.98	22.91	+0.93
20.	Kota	8.14	0.11	1.22	18.94	12.16	−6.78
21.	Nagaur	7.57	2.53	3.40	27.00	23.99	−3.01
22.	Pali	5.31	1.60	1.60	17.02	39.90	+22.96
23.	S.Madhopur	7.90	0.34	1.44	19.36	12.95	−6.78
24.	Sikar	3.95	1.82	1.92	15.38	12.66	−2.72
25.	Sirohi	2.51	0.54	0.50	7.10	4.25	−2.85
26.	Tonk	5.08	1.36	0.40	13.84	11.18	−2.66
27.	Udaipur	15.88	1.33	3.27	40.96	15.80	−25.06

compels the livestock owners in general and sheep owners in particular to migrate with their flocks from fodder and water deficient area to fodder and water abundant area. Table 51 shows the migration of sheep from 9 drought affected districts as well as state as a whole from 1983-84 to 1987-88. Nearly 700,000 to 50,00,000 sheep from Western arid districts and 10,00,000 to

Table 51 : Year-wise sheep migration in Arid Districts of Rajasthan

(Thousands)

Districts	1983-84	1984-85	1985-86	1986-87	1987-88
Jaisalmer	134	69	144	375	848
Barmer	46	122	22	408	925
Jalore	48	255	29	320	355
Nagaur	253	295	165	426	976
Jodhpur	234	297	245	425	918
Bikaner	NA	NA	195	182	998
Churu	NA	NA	NA	150	76
Sikar	3	NA	26	120	NA
Jhunjhunu	NA	NA	65	70	NA
Sub Total	718	1038	891	2476	5096
	(69.30)	(71.48)	(33.08)	(65.82)	(82.22)
State Total	1036	1452	2693	3762	6199

NA Not applicable

Figures in the parenthesies are the percentages of state total

62,00,000 of sheep from the state migrated to other areas during the different periods in search of water and fodder. The migration of sheep has continuously increased from 1983-84 to 1987-88. Thus, the incidence of sheep migration in the years to come has a tendency to increase substantially.

The pastoral nomads of western Rajasthan now feel that due to pasture and water scarcity and resistance from various sources in pursuing their pastoral activities, it is difficult to build and maintain herds. The pastoralists point out that in previous generations family herds were much larger, from 400 to 600 small stock. Previously pasture was more readily available, both in home area and on migration. Now there is oposition from the agriculturists and from the Forest Department to the movement and grazing of flocks confrontations have increased, and conflicts become more frequent.

Earlier the relationship of sheep and environment, balance between pastoral nomadism and natural environment, relationship between pastoralists and sedentary peoples, cultivators, cattle owners etc. were laregly complementary. With the socio-cultural and technological transformation of the society, the functional relationship has undergone considerable changes. Symbiotic relationship between the settled non-pastoralists and the nomadic pastoralists has broken down. Settled population no longer welcomes the nomadic pastoralists. While on the move, livestock of the nomadic pastoralists is associated with the destructive activities pertaining to soil conservation. The routes followed by the pastoralists have narrowed down due to extension of cultivation. Increase in livestock population, taking up of livestock rearing as the less risk oriented occupation by the non-livestock rearing communities, and overcrowded grazing lands have exaggerated the problems of the pastoralists.

On migration, the pastoralists are often confronted with solid agricultural fields, with no way through. Some groups are putting off migration until after the harvest, so that passage of the flocks is less problematical. Even so, the opposition from local people on the migration route, many of whom have their own livestock,is great. In the year 1983 the migratory group of Kaparada Raika ran into trouble when their animals were grazed on a harvested field without the owner's permission. This led to a stick fight with local villagers, which escalated into conflict with firearms, leading to the death of six Raika and two villagers. Now the migratory groups, **Dhung**, are formed in larger and larger size, to intimidate local people into giving access to pasture, and to protect the livestock and the herders in case of extortionate demands or direct attack by villagers on the migration route[4].

Nomadic shepherds and their animals are now increasingly unwelcome visitors to other States. A case in point is that of

Madhya Pradesh, where several clashes between nomads and foresters have been reported. Not surprising, since, according to official estimates, one millon sheep, goats, camels and cattle from Rajasthan graze in Madhya Pradesh forests every year.

Livestock from other states passing through Madhya Pradesh are given transit passes, and the shepherds are supposed to ensure that their animals do not linger on to graze. However, following complaints that the transit passes were being abused the Madhya Pradesh government in 1979 drastically amended rules: it prescribed a steep grazing fee of Rs. 25 for outside sheep as against Re.one for 'local' sheep and fixed a limit of 45 days for livestock to pass through the state.

The nomads went to court, arguing in a writ petition before the Supreme Court that the order constituted a breach of fundamental rights and was discriminatory in several other ways. In May 1983, the court decided in their favour, upholding their right to graze cattle, sheep and camels in transit to other States and holding the higher charges for 'outside' animals unconstitutional. The court remarked that "no Indian is a foreigner in any of the constitutent States", "it cannot be that the Madhya Pradesh cattle are less destructive than the cattle belonging to persons of other States", and that the higher rates only favoured the rich. The court also struck down the 45 day rule but held the government's prescription of a route for the nomadic livestock as a reasonable restriction.

The tension continued, however. In August 1983, a contingnent of 70 forest officials swooped down on a group of shepherds, Rewaris from Gujarat, grazing their herds in Khandwa district. The operation lasted six hours, left 185 sheep dead--the Rewaris claim 250—and two injured shepherds. The foresters claimed the shepherds were there illegally. The shepherds charged they had applied for transit passes two months earlier but the forest department had refused to issue them without bribes. One shepherd told a reporter:"Last year we paid Rs. 5,000 extra to get 8,000 passes."

Later in September 1983 the Mandsaur district administration braced itself to prevent the entry of one million sheep and camels from Rajasthan. The warning came in a wireless message from Balkavi Balragi, Congress(I) MLA from the area and a former minister. The arrangements for the counter-offensive included the deployment of a platoon of the special armed forces and a contingent of home guards.

Following severe criticism in the press over the mass killing of sheep by forest officials in Dahinala, Balkavi Balragi, an MLA from Mandsaur wrote an angry article to the Indore daily 'Nai Duniya'. His views are a very good example of the new response of settled populations to the nomads, with their traditional ties and relations rapidly breaking down. Excerpts from Bairagi's letter :

"My own district, Mandsauar, borders the State of Rajasthan. You will find, not one or two, but three to four lakh sheep grazing in the forests here. Life has become extremely difficult for the farmers. Their crops get destroyed. Last year I had to insist with the government that police and security forces like SAF be provided for a whole month. Then only we could be liberated from the death-dance of these sheep.

"You can imagine what can happen when lakhs of sheep invade your standing crops for miles. Village after village begins to weep. Have you ever seen the preparations made by these Rajasthani shepherds to graze their sheep? They never travel alone. Fifty families travel together. They not only have guns, axes and lathis but also traditional weapons like **'gophan'**. This lump of intewoven rope is often more deadly than a gun. It is used to throw stones and if the aim is accurate, it will break your head. Round stones are thrown with it and its effectiveness depnds on the user. Good **gophan-users** can split the head of their victim half to three-quarters of a kilometre away. Our villagers are more afraid of the **gophan** than the gun. A whistling stone comes from an unknown direction and destroys its victim. Apart from this weapon, these shepherds have domesticated wild dogs, trained to hunt. An even more powerful weapon is their purse full of notes. The most powerful weapon, however, is their arrogance: We have left our house only to die. Who ever has drunk their mother's milk can come forward in front of our **gophan.**

"If you were to see the **patels** (head persons of these nomadic groups) you will get a vision of medieval lords. If a government official is able to arrest an odd group., then the head of the group will not come walking to meet him. He will either come on his camel or in his palanquin. An armed force will move with him: women armed with **gophans**, young men with guns and 50 pet dogs all around. The entire scene is so full of terror that either the man in front will faint or run for his life. These people believe that the sitting or getting down on the ground of their patel, dressed in colourful medieval clothes and bedecked with a big beard and moustache, as an equal to the person in front, is an insult to the clan-goddess. The **patel** shouts from afar: "Speak, what is your price? What is the price of your ranger? How much do we have to stick on to your DFO's beard? How hungry is your MLA? What scales do you want to weigh your minister in notes?".

"The first thing these people do on entering the forests is to announce that they will break the head of the local sarpanch. They become thirsty for his blood. If you were to feed a sheep with your own means, you will incur an expenditure of Rs.2 to Rs 4 every day. This practice of free grazing on government pastures and forests and farmers' fields by showing the lathi has always brought great economic advantages to these sheperds. In such a situation, if they have to pay a quarter or half a rupee, or even a rupee or two, they are prepared to throw the money in your face. Without any shame or embarrassment, they begin to believe that everything belongs to their forefathers, the government can be bought and the farmers' fields have been spread by God himself for their sheep. If the price cannot be negotiated, then there are **gopahans,** dogs, lathis and guns, and finally newspapers and courts.

"Last year I had about 5 lakh such sheep removed from my area. This year, at the time when the sheep were being massacred in Dahinala, policemen, panchayat and forest officials in my area were trying to rid farmers' fields of about one lakh sheep. Even Mandalgarh, the area from which Rajasthan's Chief Minister Shiv Charan Mathur comes from, has been terrorised by sheep. During the period of the Janata Government, Mathur himself was the chairman of the local 'Remove Sheep Committee' (Bhed Bhagao Samiti). Half a dozen Shepherds were killed by the local farmers that year and the Shekhawat government had filed a police report of serious offence against Mathur.

"At the moment of my writing these words, there are about 10,000 sheep grazing in my area in full freedom. Some have been chased back into Rajasthan. Some have run into Saklecha's area. This year, one forest official did an amazing thing. This petty forest official had made sufficient preparations for bloodshed all along the Rajasthan - Madhya Pradesh border. This great incarnation of God, after taking one rupee per sheep, ten rupees per camel and five rupees per donkey, gave grazing permits to thousands of sheep to graze anywhere in all of Madhya Pradesh. Grazing was permitted not just for 10 or 20 days, but uptil 1984. These permits are invalid and illegal. But when the forest officials and policemen on my insistence went to act against the shepherd, they threw these permits in their face.

"For a whole fortnight these nomads terrorised the place. They even did criminal things like snatching money from people walking along the roads and snatching rotis from mothers and sisters going to the fields. They began to hunt for every sarpanch and threaten him with his blood. The terrorised villagers came to me. I met the local district magistrate and superintendent of police. It was fortunate that I found two officials who fully understood this problem in Mandsaur district. They helped us fully. Even today a police patrol is active.

"You may or may not know, but these grazing and transit passes do not give permission for grazing in reserve forests. But once inside the forest, who knows what is a grazing forest and what is a reserve forest? Permission is granted to 10,000 sheep but 2 lakh sheep enter, if you can count, you are welcome to do so. They will point towards the sheep grazing for miles in forests and farmed fields and say: 'Eight thousand are already grazing here. Another herd of 2,000 will come in a day or two. Why don't you come back then and count? Few people know how difficult it is to count lakhs of sheep in a forest. Even more difficult is the behaviour of the sheep. This is a very obstinate animal. It obeys its master. If the shepherd has asked it to sit, then it will give its life, but it will not get up. Forest officials and villagers kill it only in their bid to pick it up or remove it. The shepherd simply gives the sheep his command and sits down to smoke his hookah in peace.

The conflict between the pastoral nomads and the local villagers especially of Jhalawar, Bhilwara, Bundi, Kota, Chittorgarh, districts in Rajasthan has assumed serious dimension, and every year it has become a law and order problem for the administration of these districts. This conflict has been increasing since 1979. In the following statment, a chronology of the various conflicts that arose between the pastoral nomads and the local people between 1979 and 1988 is given. It may be seen from the statement that the conflict has been taking place largely in the districts of Chittorgarh, Bhilwara, Bundi and Kota. Another important feature of the conflict is that these take place mostly in the month of July - August when the first monsoon rains come and the sheep farmers start returning to their home villages through these districts.

The statement showing conflict between sheep farmers and local cattle owners.

Year	District	Villages	Consequences of Conflict			
			Sheep	Farmer	Local owners	Cattle
			Injury	Death	Injury	Death
1979-80	Chittorgarh	Kalayanpur,Khokda Ka Jungale,Gopal-pura,Bawri Khera	2	–	3	–
1981-82	Bhilwara	Daulatpura,Khabaria, Chileswar,Jityas	–	–	12	–
	Chittorgarh	Khakri ka Jungale	2	–	–	–
1982-83	Chittorgarh	Nagawali	–	–	1	–
1983-84	Chitorgarh	Eto ka Talab Ghagarmaru	15	–	–	–
1987	Baundi	Sagha	2	–	–	–
		Khandipur	1	3	–	–
		Gadba	8	2	–	–
	Kota	Jumbudip	4	1	–	–
	Chittorgarh	Baritash	3	–	6	–
	Chittorgarh	Nimpuria	–	1	–	–

Source: Sheep & Wool Directorate, Govt. of Rajasthan, Jaipur.

The cattle owners of these districts complain that the new grasses which grow after falling of monsoon rains are eatenup hurriedly by the migratory flocks, thus leaving no grass for our own cattle. When we resist the movement of the migratory flocks, the flockowners indulge in quarrels with us which ultimately leads to stick fights and attacks with firearms causing grievous injuries and deaths to members of both the sides.

In the first week of July the migratory sheep enter Rajasthan from various places and follow the following traditional routes to reach their destination in the various districts.

I. Sikri (U.P), Karauli, Kailadevi, Sapotra, Indergarh, Nainwa, Bundi, Beeswamile (Bundi), Bijolia (Bhilwara)

II. Gwalior, Morena (M.P), Dholpur, Mandrail (Sawai Madhopur)

III. Bijapur, Sabalgarh (M.P.), Dholpur, Mandrail (Sawai Madhopur)

IV. Sheopur (M.P.), Dhebri, Indergarh, Nainwa, Bundi,

V. Shivpuri, Goras (M.P), Mangrole, Indergarh, Nainwa, Bundi, Beeswamile, Bijolia.

VI. Ashoknagar (M.P), Kasbathana, Sahabad, Mangrole, Indergarh, Nainwa, Bundi, Beeswamile, Bijolia.

VII. Guna(M.P), Nahargarh, Bhanwargarh, ABaran, Kota, Palka (Bundi).

VIII. Chachoda (M.P), Manoharthana, Eklera, Patan.

IX. Khilchipura (M.P), Bhojpur, Eklera, Bakani.

X. Susner (M.P) Raipur, Patan, Sagod, Kota, Khanpur, Mandawar and Patan.

XI. Bhanpura (M.P), Rawatbhata, Bhensrorgarh, Tilasmia Mahadeo (Bhilwara).

XII. Mandsaur, Neemuch (M.P), Nimbahera, Chittorgarh, Begun Mandsaur, Pratapgarh, Bansi, Chhotisadri.

The problem faced by the pastoral nomads during rainy season have been receiving special attention of the Government of Rajasthan since 1978. In the year 1980, an action plan to control the sheep migration in consultation with the concerned District Collectors and other officials was made. So far the breeders had taken their sheep flocks in a set direction according to their discretion. But in the year 1980 efforts were made to regulate their movement to avoid heavy concentration in some districts by fixing the number of sheep which could be permitted to graze in different areas of each district. The action plan proposed to regulate the sheep migration is given below.

S.No.	Name of district	Name of places	Traditional concentration	Proposed sheep number for grazing
I.	Bhilwara	1. Bhopatpyra, Chhoti Bijolia	30,000	10,000
		2. Bijolia	20,000	10,000
		3. Ladpura	20,000	10,000
		4. Tilsmia Mahadeo	20,000	5,000
		5. Salawatia	20,000	10,000
		6. Joganiamata	15,000	5,000
			1,25,000	50,000
II.	Chittor	1. Chotisadri	30,000	15,000
		2. Pratapgarh	30,000	20,000
		3. Rawatbhata	25,000	20,000
		4. Bijapura	15,000	15,000
			1,00,000	70,000
III.	Udaipur	1. Gogunda	5,000	30,000
		2. Jhadol	3,000	30,000
		3. Kotra	5,000	10,000
		4. Pamarwa	-	15,000
			13,000	85,000
IV.	Bundi	1. Indergarh	15,000	10,000
		2. Bundi-Beeswamile	30,000	10,000
		3. Chandmari, Palka Dabi	30,000	10,000
			75,000	30,000
V.	Jhalawar	1. Bakani, Manoharthana	30,000 (Rajasthani) 75,000 (Kuchchi) (Gujrat)	20,000
VI.	Kota	1. Durra	25,000 (Rajasthani) 50,000 (Kunchi) (Gujrat)	15,000
		2. Atru	20,000	15,000

(*Contd.*)

S.No.	Name of district	Name of places	Traditional concentration	Proposed sheep number for grazing
		3. Chhabra	10,000	5,000
			25,000	35,000
VII.	Sawaimadhopur			
		1. Karauli	50,000	30,000
		2. Kailadevi Sapotra	50,000	45,000
		3. Mandrail	30,000	30,000
		4. Debri	20,000	5,000
			1,50,000	1,10,000
		Total	5,48,000	4,00,000

In order to minimize the concentration of sheep the following diversion points had been fixed:-

S. No.	Name of district	Diversion Point	Number of diverted	sheep to be
1.	Bhilwara	(i) Indergarh	20,000 to	Indergarh/ Sheopur
		(ii) Kota Barrage	25,000 to	Durra Manoharthana
		(iii) Nimbahera	15,000 to	Mangelwad Jhadol
		(iv) Pratapgarh	15,000 to	Bansi/Dhariwad & Panarwa
			75,000	
2.	Chittor	(i) Nimbahera to Jhadol via Udaipur	10,000 to	Jhadol
		(ii) Pratapgarh	10,000 to	Deogarh, Dhariwad & Jhadol
		(iii) Rawantbhata	10,000 to	Kota via Durra
			30,000	

(*Contd.*)

S. No.	Name of district		Diversion Point	Number of sheep to be diverted	
3.	Udaipur	(i)	Ratlam, Sailana (checkpost) Banswara, Arthana Galiakot, Sagwara Dungarpur, Daval, Kherwara, Bavalwara Som and Kotra.	10,000	
		(ii)	Prataphar, Dhariwad, Bawalwara, Som Panarwa	15,000	
		(iii)	Nimbahera, Chittor Mangalwar Betaver, Daroli, Udaipur, Undri, Jhadol.	30,000	
		(iv)	Rawatbhata Bhensrorgarh, Begu, Bassi, Gangrar, Kapasan, Railmangora, Nathdwara, Khamor & Gogunda.	30,000	
4.	Blundi	(i)	Indergarh	15,000 to	Mangrol, Shiv-puri(MP)
		(ii)	Durra	15,000 to	Patan
		(iii)	Kota	15,000 to	Durra Patan
				45,000	
5.	Jhalawar	(i)	Manoharthana	5,000 to	Chadhoda (M.P)
		(ii)	Eklera	3,000 to	Khilchipur (M.P)
		(iii)	Dug	2,000 to	Agar (M.P)
				10,000	
6.	Kota	(i)	Mangrole	10,000 to	Goras (M.P)
		(ii)	Durra	10,000 to	Patan, Man-oharthana,Chan-choda (M.P.)
7.	Sawaimadhopur				
		(i)	Mandrail	10,000 to	Sabalgarh(M.P)
		(ii)	Dhebri	10,000 to	Sheopur (M.P)
		(iii)	Dhebri	10,000 to	Indergarh, Mangrole, Sheopur (M.P)
		(iv)	Mandrail	10,000 to	Bijapur (M.P)

The Collector, Udaipur had constituted a committee constiting of District Sheep & Wool Officer, concerned Tehsildar and Block Development Officer to detail out the villages which would fall on these and finalise route with the consultation of the non-officials. During the year 1991-92, the Sheep & Wool Department, Government of Rajasthan fixed the following number of sheep to be permitted for entering into the following 9 districts duuring monsoon period.

Sl.No.	District	No.of Sheep permitted (1991-92)
1.	Bhilwara	80,000
2.	Chittorgarh	1,40,000
3.	Bundi	1,10,000
4.	Jhalawar	1,10,000
5.	Sawai Madhopur	1,50,000
6.	Kota	1,90,000
7.	Udaipur	1,40,000
8.	Alwar	90,000
9.	Dholpur	80,000

The sheep and wool department has established 41 check-posts on inter-state border to regulate the sheep migration in districts. (See Annexure-II) Government of Rajasthan has also formed a committee under the chairmanship of Chief Secretary including the officers of Police, Forests and other related departments. This committee generally meets every year in April-May and fixes approximately the number of migratory animals for each district. Regular meetings are arranged with villagers and migratory flockowners in the sensitive districts for preventing any quarrel amongst them. The sheep and wool department has also issued identity cards to each **numberdar,** chief of the migratory group, in which the number of the sheep and the route, which will follow, will be mentioned. Again at the diversion check-post an entry is made in the identity card to indicate his diversion route which he must follow to reduce the concentration[5].

These measures have no doubt helped in reducing the tensions between the pastoral nomads and the local cattle owners in the sensitive districts as no case of conflict was reported during the year 1989 and 1990. But delay caused in making various entries in the identity cards at the various diversion check posts often causes lot of discomforts to the pastoral nomads. Sometimes they have to wait for about 5 to 6 days near the check posts for getting necessary entries made in the identity cards. Near the check posts there is no grazing land and hence the flocks have either to starve or enter into somebody's agricultural fields or protected forests to graze. This leads to conflict with the cultivators and the Forest Department. This can be avoided by making speedy entries in the identity cards of the nomads at the check-posts.

Besides conflict with the stationery flock-owners, the pastoral nomads also face problems with regard to the security of the flocks and property of the flockowners. The nomads migrating to the State of Uttar Pradesh from Rajasthan State said that in the districts of Mainpuri, Eta, Etawa, Agra and Farukhabad of Uttar Pradesh, organised gangs of dacoits loot their animals and property. Even in the **daangs** of Rajasthan, dacoits loot their animals and property. Similary, the pastoral nomads of Gujarat complained that in places like Malia, Viramgaon and Dangedara the thiefs of Dafer community, often armed with guns, also loot their animals and property thus causing economic loss to them. As a solution the pastoral nomads suggested that if they could get licenses for keeping guns, then this would at least help in intimidating the thieves and dacoits.

Rangelands degradation

Ecological degradation of modern times as we see is not due to any climatic shift but is man made. We have today 400 million of domestic grazing animals against a human population of 800 million. Livestock is the most important consumer group of the ecosystem. Rough calculation shows that 117 million ha. of grazing lands serve about 400 million of domestic animals. So it works out to nearly 3.3 animals/ha. It is true that the cow unit equivalence is not worked out but taking into acount the larger and smaller animals the average herbage requirement may be about the same as for cows of the totalled number.

With the advent of civilisation the pastoral economy gradually developed into agricultural economy with livestock rearing a major component. Gradually as the human population increased the grazing areas were brought under cultivation of food crops as a result the grazing pressure increased on forest areas manifold. Besides the large bovine population their continuous and close grazing in and outside the forests have resulted in the degradation of forests. The palatable and nutritious grasses are getting replaced by the less palatable and inferior grasses. Areas got invaded by unwanted and unpalatable bushes and weeds like **Lantana camara, Dodonnea, Parthenium** etc. Thereby even the grassland areas have further decreased by 30 to 40% from the net available area increasing thereby more pressure of grazing on the remaining forest areas.

Between 1951 and 1981, while the area under agriculture increased by 13.4 per cent, livestock population increased by 42-53 per cent resulting in overgrazing and fast degradation of forest areas. The degradation in range health is so acute that just to support one adult cattle 10-15 ha of rangelands are required in semiarid and arid zones.

Our rangelands are severly exposed to exploitation due to indiscriminate and over grazing as a result of heavy livestock pressure. Increasing human population and their growing needs have further deteriorated these lands by indiscriminate removal of bushes, feeling of trees thus disturbing the ecosystem. Over grazing induces secondary succession and ultimately to desertification. It becomes very expensive or impossible to put back the wasteland into pasturelands[6].

Experts meeting at the U.N. conference on desrtification in Nairobi in 1977 had agreed unanimously that nomadism and transhumance animal husbandry is ecologically sound practise of migration of livestock from degraded environment to other productive zones. But this migration system, as felt by the Forest Department, Government of Madhya Pradesh, is not applicable with regard to western Madhya Pradesh. The area is already under rehabilitation. In this part the forests and pasture lands have disappeared. It is itself an "ecologically fragile zone". The migration of herds and flocks particularly from drought prone and desert areas had led to hapazard grazing, putting too much pressure on insufficient grazing lands. How a State which has a huge deficit of 46.9 per cent in respect of dry fodder and 74.7 per cent in green fodder is expected to feed millions of unwelcome sheep, goats, camels and cattle from adjoining States? The State can sustain only a third of its livestock population. The current fodder crisis can only aggravate the problem further if millions of migratory livestock are allowed to graze on it.

A study conducted by **Kalla** and **Gupta**[7] on the sheep and land use in Western Rajasthan revealed the rise in sheep population required annual availability of fodder from 11 to 15 million tonnes. This needed earmarking 4.4 to 6 million hectares annually for fodder production. But in the absence of any systematic forage production, the pressure has come on to the forests where the grazing animals have plundered the natural regeneration and the forests to thinned and degraded. As per the existing forage resources, the stocking rate is almost 4 to 6 times heavier than what rangelands and forests are capable of sustaining. Consequently, continued overutilization of range and forest resources by nomadic stockowners has led to depletion of the original climax or sub-climax vegetation, accelerating thereby the process of soil erosion, sanddune formation and loss of soil fertility **(Das and Paroda)**[8].

By the year 1986 the attitude towards sheep and goat grazing in the forests became so hostile that in the meeting of Doon valley on 22nd September, 1986 it was considered to discontinue the distribution of sheep and goat under the Integrated Rural Development Programme (IRDP) in the ecologically fragile zones. Subsequently a Task Force Under the Chairmanship of Prof. C.H.Hanumantha Rao was constituted on 28th January, 1987 to evaluate the impact of sheep and goat rearing in ecologically fragile zone. The committee in its report observed that sheep and goats do not pose a threat to the ecology as is generally believed. In any case,their negative effect, if any, on ecology has been vastly exaggerated. On the other hand, they make a very important contribution to the survival of economically weaker section of our society and for meeting the requirements of industry, besides earning valuable foreign exchange through exports. A comparative study of sheep and goat rearing and of cattle in ecologically fragile zone, according to Task Force Report, indicates that within the desired grazing pressure, sheep and goats are more economical and less harmful than large ruminants.

In a rejoinder to the Task Force Report, Mr. Ram Prasad, Director, State Forest Research Institute, Jabalpur, Madhya Pradesh criticised the findings of the Task Force and wrote that their arguments, however, do not appear to be based on any scientific studies as no such references have been quoted in support of their contentions. Perusal of scant bibilography given on page 51 of this report shows references on economic aspects of goat and sheep rearing. Scanning of world literature would reveal that almost all the studies and observations have described the disastrous effect of grazing by livestock in general and goats and sheep in particular. Dr Ram Prasad gave following examples to support his views. "It would be of common knowledge that many Muslim Countries in Asia have banned sheep and goats in view of their well known role in creating deserts and destroying many civilizations. Cases of Mesopotamia, Babylonia and others are well documented where destruction of forests led to the devastation and consequent wiping out of civilization."

The Hanumantha Rao Committee report (page 21, para 2) states: "Grazing as such is not inimical to forest growth: in fact, light grazing improves regeneration conditions, particularly in moist type of forests". However, learned members of the Committee have probably not taken into account the ecological disaster which western and eastern Himalayas have faced on account of grazing and other human acts. Forest destruction in Cherapunji is a typical case where despite being the wettest part of the country has failed to respond to healing through reforestation.

Subsequent assertions are based on National Forest Policy which was enacted about four decades ago and National Commission on Agriculture (NCA) report which made projections about decades ago appear to have become outdated as probably our planners might not have visualised the pace of forest destruction as a result of excessive biotic pressure would be so fast and devastating. Even then on the basis of observations in Europe, Australia and America, the RCA had held that the grazing of inferior cattle in the forests should be discouraged. This report itself has quoted the judicious caution spelled out by RCA and NCA (1976) about the harmful effects of excessive grazing in forests.

However, in subsequent para this report takes a philosophical view about forest degradation stating that this is not due to sheep and goats. This is far from the truth and none of the reported cases in our report favours grazing in forests by goats and sheep.

Perusal of land use statistics in India would clearly reveal that while area under agriculture continued increasing steadily the areas under permanent pasture, grazing and forests continued shrinking. It would be worth mentioning here that loss of area from forests and grazing land has mostly been accounted for by ever expanding agriculture. While these areas under permanent vegetation continued shrinking the population of man and his animals recorded unprecedented increase. All scientific evidences reveal that our forests have been getting thinned mostly on account of excessive grazing, browsing and trampling. Even if man burnt forests to ensure luxuriant grass growth it was meant for his livestock.

Under "Summary and Recommendations" (p 6, Sr.2 of the report) it is recommended that:

(2) "The grazing habits, total phytomass consumption, return to organic matter from sheep and goats to the soil etc. were studied and compared with other ruminant like cattle, buffaloes, antelope etc. It could not be established that sheep and goats are responsible for the degradation of ecology. It is therefore, recommended that these animals should not be categorised as animals responsible for the destruction of ecology."

(3) "A comparative study of sheep and goat rearing and of cattle in ecologically fragile zones indicate that, within the desired grazing pressure, sheep and goats are more economical and less harmful than large ruminants."

Perusal of these two recommendations of the task force would at first instance give an impression that sheep and goats grazing in forests and permanent pastures are not at all inimical. These may also mislead the readers that the committee has either relied upon some published scientific evidence or have over a number of years, carried out research to arrive at these conclusions. However, none of the two assumptions could be true as neither the Committee refers to any such works not they have carried out experiments on any such aspects. Further, on the basis of findings of long drawn research programmes and field observations world over, the scientists and foresters have unequivocally shown the correlation between destruction of permanent vegetation and rampant grazing in excess of its carrying capacity by all kinds of livestock. Sheep and goats have been said to be just like "**Cancer of earth**" as they wipeout the vegetation indiscriminately. Eminent ecologists like Odum and experts like R.O. Whyte have also attributed the reasons for ecological imbalances to over grazing in general and grazing by sheep and goats in particular.

NCA Report (1976) mentions about the causes of forest degradation in hilly areas (42.10.3 page 125). In that it is mentioned "It has been generally recognized that in the hilly areas the genesis of soil and water erosion problems usually lies in either the indiscriminate felling of trees or in the overgrazing of pasture lands." The loss of vegetative cover in such areas as a result of indiscriminate overgrazing by migratory herds of camels, cattle, sheep and goats has exposed top soil to erosion by strong winds. The ravines in Uttar Pradesh, Madhya Pradesh, Rajasthan and Gujarat are also caused by felling of trees and overgrazing. The areas categoriesed as "Permanent pastures and other grazing lands" covering about 13 million hectares perhaps represent, fallaciously though, some of the worst eroded areas. Whether it is the pasture lands of the desert or of the high hills, they are characterised by unchecked misuse. Grazing is by and large unrestricted in forest areas, the livestock feeding on undergrowth and trespassing into the young regenerated areas. This type of indiscriminate grazing reduces the capacity of forests to conserve soil and moisture".

"Grazing in the Forests": NCA Report 1976 (p 132), states, the national forest policy should recognize that grazing in the forests would have to be allowed in view of the role of livestock in the country's economy. But instead of unlimited and continuous grazing, it should be controlled and restricted so that it does not interfere with the productive and protective functions of the forests. ...... Grazing by goats in all forests should be prohibited. Sheep grazing may be allowed only in specially earmarked grasslands in the forest areas under strict rotational control.

Dr. Voelcker's Report and 1894 Forest Policy regarding Grazing:

... "I can quite understand, too the damage that will be done to a forest where reproduction is going on either on account of cattle trampling down the seedlings, or by goats and sheep nibbling off young shoots. Goats, in particular, must have no place in a forest of this kind.".....

Govt. of India accepted his recommendations and accordingly categorized the forests.

Views of the Royal Commission on Agriculture:

"It is desirable, in the interests both of forest conservancy and of cattle improvement, that the grazing of inferior cattle in the forests should be discouraged. In all cases, the aim should be to secure a due proportion of grass cutting to grazing in each forest tract."

Forest Grazing in National Forest Policy, 1952:

(i) Continuous grazing on the same areas by large herds is destructive to the better strains of grasses and leads to a deterioration of the grass complex. Wherever it is permitted and is in great demand, efforts should be made to introduce rotational grazing, the benefits of which should be explained and demonstrated to the villagers.

(ii) Cheap forest grazing has a demoralising effect and leads to the vicious spiral of reckless increase in the number of cattle, inadequate forest grazing, reduced quality of herds and further increase in the numbers to offset the fall in quality. Free and indiscriminate forest grazing is, therefore, a serious disservice to cattle breeding. The notion that a farmer's wealth must be reckoned in terms of the cattle he owns, regardless of quality, is one of the causes of India's uneconomic cattle wealth and must be combated.

(iii) Grazing should not be looked upon primarily as a source of revenue. But the simple and obvious way of regulating and controlling grazing, as also improving the quality both of grazing and cattle themselves, is to institute a reasonable fee for the privilege of grazing.

(iv) Grazing must not be allowed in regeneration areas and young plantations during such periods as the seedlings require for establishment.

(v) Grazing incidence should be kept at a minimum in protection forests i.e those forests which must be preserved or created for physical and climatic considerations.

The National Forest Policy, 1952 stated that the damage to young plants caused by the browsing of sheep and goats is often irreparable, and their admission into forests is incompatible with the aims and objects of forest management. Experience gained in India and elsewhere points to the imposition of restrictions on sheep grazing in forests, and the total exclusion of goats therefrom.

The Task Force Report has however, made a surmise that sheep and goats were introduced in arid and semi-arid regions of Rajasthans and Gujarat at some stage indicating that fragility or xerification existed and have not been caused by sheep and goats. However, the members have not considered the fact that these two States are mostly forestless. Rajasthan has maximum wastelands in the country. There is no other State having same ecological crisis as are being faced by Rajasthan and Gujarat State. These facts bear testimony to the excessive biotic pressures which have created desert like conditions in these two States. It is also to be noted that the ecological decay has also spread to adjoining areas of Madhya Pradesh, more so in the northern and western parts of the State where on account of large scale influx of nomadic, sheep, goats, camels and other ruminants have destroyed the forests. The process of ecological devastation in northern and western Madhya Pradesh, adjoining Rajasthan and Gujarat, have been more pronounced in past two decades or so[9].

Silvicultural conferences are held regularly at Forest Research Institute (FRI), Dehradun, the highest national body for forestry research. These conferences have been making suitable recommendations for implementation by State Forest Departments. Some recommendations are as follows :

Eighth Silvicultural Conference

(ii) the incidence of grazing be limited to the carrying capacity of the pasture which should be correctly determined.

Ninth Silvicultural Conference:

(a) Excessive grazing by domestic animals is incompatible with sound forestry practice and ultimately destroys the grazing capacity of the land;

(b) Of the various domestic animals in India, the goat is the most destructive and as pointed out by previous conferences and other authorities, should be kept out of forests;

(c) State Governments be approached urgently to take more effective steps to limit cattle grazing in forest areas to the actual carrying capacity of the land and to seriously discourage if not totally eliminate goat grazing.

Tenth Silvicultural Conference:

(a) Grazing is a serious problem in forest areas in many States and is often very deterimental to the regeneration of forest species;

From the above accounts, reports and conferences it has been brought out that excessive grazing in forests has led to the destruction of habitat. Further, grazing by goats and sheep should not be permitted in forests as they destroy forest regeneration which is so essential for the continuance of the forest ecosystem. It is to be remembered that the pastoral nomads have been continuing with their sheep husbandry economy against all these strong and negative feelings about the impact of sheep and goats grazing on the forests. The sheep farmers have been receiving very hostile treatments at the hands of various Forest Department Officials. Not only they have to face inhuman treatment, and abusive remarks from the Forest Department staff but also quite often they are forced to pay heavy bribes to the Forest Officials for grazing in the forests. It is said that every year the Forest Department officials eagerly await the arrival of the migratory shepherds to make huge money by accepting bribe and illegally allowing the flockowners to graze in the reserved forests.

With a view to restrict the movements of the migratory shepherds and their flocks in the forests of Madhya Pradesh, the Government of Madhya Pradesh suddenly increased the grazing fee per cattle/sheep/goat from 0.25 paise to Re. 1 in 1974 and then from Re.1/- to Rs. 5/- per sheep especially for the migratory flocks which they labelled as foreign cattle. They also prescribed the routes for the foreign cattle and stipulated that these cattle must leave Madhya Pradesh within 45 days. This decision was challenged in the Supreme court of India which in its judgement quashed the levy of higher grazing rates in the case of cattle belonging to persons other than State of Madhya Pradesh and directed to levy the same rate for the migratory cattle as they do in the case of cattle belonging to residents of Madhya Pradesh. The limit of stay of 45 days was also declared unconstitutional.

After their failure before the Supreme Court in the above case, the government of Madhya Pradesh became extremely hostile to the nomadic graziers, and started adopting a revengeful attitude. The Madhya Pradesh Government framed the Madhya Pradesh grazing Rules, 1986 (See Annexure-III) and raised the grazing rates. The grazing rate for sheep, which was Re.1/- per sheep in 1979, was raised to Rs.10/- per sheep. This was again challenged in the High Court of Madhya Pradesh at Jabalpur. This raising of grazing fee was also criticised by various Members of Parliament, Union Ministers, Chief Ministers of Rajasthan and Gujarat and several Senior Officers of the Central Government. As a result, the Government of Madhya Pradesh in the month of August, 1989 reduced the grazing rate by 20%. Later an amendment was made in the Madhya Pradesh Grazing Rules 1986 on 9 January, 1991. According to the amendment, the revised annual grazing fees have been fixed as per the rate given below :

(a) **Cattle Units owned by a villager:-**	
(i) Cows, Bulls, Bullocks :	Rs. Nil
(ii) Others Cattle	
(a) Up to 20 cattle units :	Rs.Nil
(b) **21 to 31 cattle units** :	Rs. 4.00 per Cattle Unit
(c) **More than 30 cattle units** :	Rs. 8.00 per Cattle Unit
(i) Cow, Bulls, Bullocks :	Rs.Nil
(ii) Other cattle :	Rs. 8.00 per cattle unit.

The 20% reduction in the grazing rates by the Madhya Pradesh Government has not made pastoral nomads happy as they feel that it is very exorbitant. After paying this heavy grazing fees, the pastoralists are not able to save much money. Further more, these grazing rates are much higher than the grazing rates in other States which are given in Table 52.

The pastoral nomads who graze their cattle in Madhya Pradesh also complained that many a times they were forced by the Forest Department Officials to pay grazing fees separately in different districts. This practise was not correct which, however, was rectified by the Government of Madhya Pradesh by issuing an order on 26 September, 1990 for collecting the grazing fee only once from the migratory shepherds. During my discussions with the pastoral nomads in Madhya Pradesh it was further revealed that for the last 3 to 4 years, the forest officials, in order to harass the pastoral nomads and to realise bribes, had either stopped taking grazing fees or giving proper receipts for grazing fees. This practise was causing problems to the nomads as this gave opportunity to the forest officials to exploit and harass the nomads in several ways.

Table 52: Grazing Rates In Forests Of Different States

Sl. No.	State	Grazing Rates for Different Animals (Rs.)						
		Sheep	Goat	Camel	Cow	Buffaloe	Horse	Donkey
1.	Rajasthan	0.50	0.50	2.00	2.00	5.00	2.00	1.00
2.	Gujarat	0.13	0.13	2.00	–	–	–	–
3.	Maharashtra	1.00	1.00	2.00	–	–	–	–
4.	Orissa	0.30	0.30	2.00	–	–	–	–
5.	Uttar Pradesh							
	(a) Local Cattle	1.00	1.00	5.00	–	–	–	–
	(b) Migratory	Nil	Nil	Nil	Nil	Nil	Nil	Nil
6.	Haryana	Nil	Nil	Nil	Nil	Nil	Nil	Nil
7.	Punjab	Nil	Nil	Nil	Nil	Nil	Nil	Nil
8.	Madhya Pradesh	8.00	8.00	40.00	–	–	–	–

Pastoral Nomads Organization

Prior to 1980, pastoral nomads did not have any registered organization of their own. It was only in October, 1980 that an organization of the pastoral nomads was formed and registered under section 6 of the **Rajasthan Co-operative Societies Act, 1965.**

It is known as Rajasthan Ghumakkar Bhedpalak Sahkari Samiti Ltd. Rajasthan Nomadic Shepherds Co-operative Society, however, has remained dormant ever since its inception due to leadereship, organizational management and financial problems.

Although the registered Co-operative Society of the pastoral nomads failed to contribute anything significant, the regional informal organization of the pastoral nomads have done commendable work since 1974 in fighting injustices against them and articulating their problems before the Government, State Legislatures and Indian Parliament. In fact, the writ petition in the Supreme Court of India and in the High Court of Madhya Pradesh at Jabalpur against the hike in grazing rates and discrimination between the local cattle owners and the migratory shepherds in Madhya Pradesh was filed on behalf of the informal and unregistered nomad's organizations which are divided into the following four regional segments.

1. **Godwad Ghumakkar (Nomadic) Bhedpalak(Sheep-rearers) Sangh (Organization)**

This organization is headed by Mr. Bajaji and represents the pastoral nomads inhabiting the districts of Barmer, Jalore, Sirohi, half area of Pali and Jodhpur. These districts collectively are known as **GODWAD** region.

2. **Maru or Karal Ghumakkar Bhedpalak Sangh**

It includes Districts of 1/2 area of Pali, Ajmer, Bhilwara, 1/2 area of Jodhpur and 1/4th area of Nagaur. This organization is headed by Mr. Harji.

3. **Nagaur Ghumakkar Bhedpalak Sangh**

It includes only Nagaur District and is headed by Mr. Ram Pallava.

4. **Kuchchi Ghumakkar Bhedpalak Sangh**

This organization represents the pastoral nomads of 64 villages of Kuchch district of Gujarat state and is headed by Mr. Laxman.

Unfortunately all these 4 organizations are unregistered and faced with the common problems of dynamic leadership, organizational management, poor communication and co-ordination, illiteracy and awareness about legal procedure, etc. Fortunately, these 4 regional organization of the pastoral nomads had a very dynamic Honorary Secretary Mr. Dalel Singh Rathore, who retired as District Sheep & Wool Officer, Jaipur. Mr. Rathore who had not only a sympathetic and friendly attitude towards these pastoral nomads, but also profound experience about their problems, played a key role in fighting the problems of pastoral nomads.

All these four organizations together presented a memorandum on 27 Feb. 1989 to the Late Prime Minister of India, Mr. Rajiv Gandhi regarding problems of pastoral nomads (See Annexure - III). As a result of the actions taken on this memorandum, a National Workshop on Sheep Migration was organised from 6 - 7 February, 1991 at Jaipur in which following 5 organizations collaborated.

1. Central Sheep & Wool Research Institute
2. Rajasthan Sheep & Wool Development Department
3. Rajasthan State Co-operative Sheep & Wool Marketing Federation.
4. Wool Development Board.
5. Indian Society for Sheep & Wool Production & Utilization.

The Workshop was attended by 91 paraticipants comprising scientists, economists, foresters, administrators and pastoral nomads. The workshop came out with 13 recommendations for solving the problems of sheep migration (See Annexure -IV).

Reduction In Grazing Areas Due to Afforestation

In order to increase the forest cover and to raise the standard of living of the people of desert, National Agriculture Commission (1976) had recommended for large scale afforestation and pasture development works to be undertaken in desert. In the year 1978 Directorate for Afforestation and Pasture Development was established with a view to executing the forestry works in the desert area. In 11 arid districts of Western Rajasthan, afforestation work under Desert Development Programme was started. Till 1991 an area of 133552 ha. and 19269 RKM was brought under afforestation. This much of afforested area, which was earlier used for grazing of the small ruminants by the pastoral nomads and other livestock owners, have been closed for protection of the plants. This has forced the pastoral nomads to migrate to the other areas to compensate the loss of the grazing areas closed for grazing due to afforerstation programme.

Policy Issues

The Government of India has ultimately taken cognizance of the problems faced by the pastoralists with regard to grazing and livestock management. With a view to evolving a National Policy of grazing and livestock management, the Government of India, National Mission on Wasteland Development, Ministry of Environment and Forests vide its letter No. 1-32/89/TMA dated 10 January, 1990 constituted an inter-disciplinary advising group on policy issues relating to grazing and livestock management. The group was advised to consider and suggest policy prescriptions on grazing, fodder production and livestock management with specific reference to:

(a) Management of Common grazing

(b) Grazing on Forest Lands

(c) Review of grazing and grass-cuttings rights on common lands and forest lands

(d) Development of silvipasture in forest areas to meet local demand.

(e) Supplementary fodder production strategy from agricultural lands.

(f) Organisational linkages between the concerned Central Ministries/Department and the State Departments with regard to research, extenstion, infrastructural and other support.

Although the report of the advisory group has been submitted to the Government of India, its recommendation are yet being discussed by various other experts and representatives of the State Governments, and have not been declared open for circulation. It is sincerely hoped that the recommendations of the advisory group when implemented, would provide relief to the pastoral nomads from their problems.

REFERENCES

1. Salzman, Philip Carl. 1986. Shrinking Pasture for Rajasthani Pastoralists. In **Nomadic Peoples.** Commission on Nomadic Peoples, IUAES, No. 20.
2. Ibid.
3. Bose, A.B. 1975. Pastoral Nomadism in India. In **Pastoralists and Nomads in South Asia,** L.S.Leshnik and G.D.Sontheimer, editors Weisbaden : Otto Harrassowitz.
4. Op.cit. Salzman, Philip Carl. 1986.
5. The State of India's Environment 1984-85. The Second Citizens Report. **Centre for Science and Environment,** New Delhi. 1985.
6. Singh, Punjab. 1988. Indian Rangelands Status and Improvement. **Plenury address -- Third International Range land Congress.** New Delhi.
7. Kalla, J.C and B.S Gupta. 1980. Growth of Sheep Population and Landuse Policy Implication in Arid Zone of Western Rajasthan. **Ann. Arid Zone** 19(3) : 345 - 350.
8. Das, R.B. and R.S. Paroda. 1980 Rational Utilization of Grazing Resources for sustained Primary and Secondary Productivity in Arid Zone of Western Rajasthan. **Ann. Arid Zone** 19(4) : 407-412.
9. Prasad, Ram and P. Bhatnagar. 1988. Grazing in Forests : An Ecological Liability. **State Forest Research Institute**. Jabalpur (India).

7

Summary and Conclusions

Nomadism is as old as the history of mankind. Apart from the compulsions of nature and search for food, quest for knowledge and explorations of the unknown regions have led people to move from place to place and interact with different groups of people. Nomadism, though very widespread and apparently haphazard, is in reality a very specialised system, and the apparently most specialised form of nomadism is transhumance. Transhumance is the regular seasonal movement of flocks between summer and winter pastures. The main distinction between transhumance and true nomadism is not that transhumance follows a fixed route, but that it involves a fixed abode for part of the year. It is defined as 'a periodic and alternating displacement of flocks between two regions of differing climate', though in fact the displacement is usually one of altitude, and is made to avoid great variations in climate.

Pastoralists are people who derive most of their income or sustenance from keeping domestic livestock in conditions where most of the feed that their livestock eat is natural forage rather than cultivated fodders and pastures. In most cases, pastoralists devote the bulk of their own, and their families working time and energy to looking after their livestock rather than to other economic activities. Pastoral areas are areas used by pastoralists and pastoralism is the term used to describe their way of life and their economic and land-use systems. Mobility is an essential feature of pastoralism.

Why some pastoralists practise nomadism? Pastoral nomadism occurs as an ecological response to an unfavourable habitat. It is practised where seasonal variations in temparature, in rainfall, in the incidence of diseases, in the growing, reopening and harvesting of crops, makes livestock-keeping in one area relatively more or less attractive than in another area according to a regular and predictable seasonal timetable. Livestock that move from one area to another according to the incidence of the rains can profit by feeding on the grazing when it is in its best condition as to palatability and protein content. Livestock may cause serious damage to crops in the cultivation zone around the pastoral areas during the growing and harvesting seasons; nevertheless they are welcome there after harvest because of their role in converting crop residues and other vegetation to manure and they can also obtain quite a high proportion of their annual feed intake there once the crops have been harvested. Nomadic movements are also made so as to produce high temporary densities of people and livestock where this is required for self-defence or because there are economies of scale. Perhaps most important of all, nomadic movements are made from one area to another because the one area has received, in this year or this season, relatively less rainfall than it normally does compared to the other.

Arid areas essentially are lands of high risk and uncertainty. Semi-arid and arid zones are climatic classifications primarily based on indices of atmospheric moisture and these are essentially water deficit zones. Those regions where only two-third of the total water need is met are arid zones. The semi-arid zones constitute 30.56% of total land area of India and are spread over 10 states. Over 70% the semiarid area is confined to the southern states and the remaining 30% lies in the western part of the north- western states.

The arid region of India covering about 3.1 lakh sq.km is roughly 12% of country's total geographical area, and is spread over 7 stataes, namely **Rajasthan, Gujarat, Haryana, Maharashtra, Karnataka, Andhra Pradesh** and portions of **Jammu and Kashmir.** The India and region lies between 24° and 29° N latitudes and 70° and 76° E longitudes. However, most (90%) of the Indian arid zone is located in north-western India. About 62% of extremely arid region is predominantly located in 11 districts **(Barmer, Bikaner,**

Churu, Jaisalmer, Jodhpur, Jalore, Jhunjhunu, Gangangar, Nagaur, Pali and Sikar) of western Rajasthan.

Pastoralism is an ecologically appropriate technique in the India landscape, which substantially consists of arid, forest and mountanious areas where agriculture occupies a marginal place. It is estimated that in India there are 50 million livestock and 34 million people managing it.

The livestock industries of arid and semi-arid zones are carried on within the limits imposed by an evnironment composed of the usual factors of climate, soil and vegetation. These general characteristics are also related to the geology and geomorphology of the site. The most important factors influencing the present nature and extent of a livestock industry and the degree to which it can be improved are, however, biotic in nature. The actual existence of man and his grazing and browsing animals in arid and semi-arid zones affects not only these habitats themselves, but also extends the area of aridity into zones which were not originally of this type. The degeneration of vegetation, however, is due as much to man's need for land for cultivation as to overgrazing. The men who live with and by livestock in arid zones are also an important, if not the dominant factor of the total environment or biome. The traditional systems of economic production, such as agriculture and pastoralism, had been well-integrated and synergistic. But with technological changes and reclamation of land for agricultural and other developmental purposes, this synergism is adversely affected. With changes in the modes of production, infusion of foreign technology and demographic pressure on land, the pastoral groups are experiencing grave consequences of impoverishment and proletarianization.

The human population of Rajasthan increased 33 per cent between 1971 and 1981 and this is a continuation of an ongoing expansion. The desert districts of Barmer, Jodhpur and Jaisalmer increased in population over the last decade 44%, 45% and 45% respectively. Taking a longer view, in Jodhpur District, the populaton increased fourfold between 1901 and 1981, from 400,000 to 1,700,000. The overall population density in Rajasthan is 100 persons per square kilometre, Jodhpur district having a density of 73 persons per sq.km. The rural population density of Jodhpur

District jumped from 34 sq.km. in 1971 to 48 per sq.km. in 1981. The last few decades have seen an unprecedented rise in the population pressure i.e from 17.2 persons per square kilometre in the year 1921 to 30.0 in 1961 and 68.4 in 1981.

Livestock population, like human population, has also increased tremendously in the last three decades in Western Rajasthan. In Rajasthan as a whole, the livestock population (mixed species) rose from 34 million in 1957 to almost 50 million in 1983, and there was an increase in livestock density from 99 per sq.km to 145 per sq.km. In the desert districts where sheep and goat predominate (over 70% of the total), the livestock numbers just about doubled between 1956 and 1983, from 800,000 to 1,500,000 to 3,500,000 in Jodhpur.

The increasing human population is a serious stress particularly on the vegetal resources of the desert. The trees and shrubs and even their roots are indiscriminately cut by the rural population for fuel, top, feed, fencing and the construction of thatched hutments. It has been estimated that the requirements of the people in the desert in respect of the woody biomass has increased from 1.85 million tonnes in 1951 to 3.33 million tonnes in 1971.

Under the influence of man when the exploitation of natural resources exceeds replacement by nature, the ecology moves towards negative side of the homeostatic plateau. Increased livestock population has got a direct correlation with the high growth rate of human population and its demand. The growth of population has affected the degree of intensity of land use by putting more sub-marginal lands under agriculture or intensive use of lands already under cultivation and intensive grazing of fastly shrinking pasture land. During the last three decades the net area sown has increased tremendously but the area under less intensive use has considerably decreased as revealed by the decline in fallow lands, wasteland and uncultivable barren wastelands. The overall grazing land has decreased significantly while the population of grazing animals has increased substantially during this period.

A positive degree of association persists between the livestock population increase and in the intensity of depletion of grazing lands. Fast increase in livestock population inspite of gradual shrinkage in the extent of grazing lands has resulted in over-exploitation of grazing lands and also to partial stravation of livestock. Consequences of too many livestock using grazing grounds are partial starving of livestock due to shortage of grasses, land getting spoiled and becoming weaker, and soil erosion due to trampling of livestock. As an adjustment mechanism, more and more pastoralist are now resorting to long distances seasonal migration, and not returning to the area along with their flocks and instead moving permanently in search of fodder in harvested fields, rangelands and forests.

The most essential things needed for livestock production are fodder, feeds, water etc. Unfortunately these are in alarmingly short supply in the arid regions of Western Rajasthan. Assessment of grazing resources availability is to be viewed in the light of the increasing livestock population and declining range productivity. The pressure of increasing livestock as expressed in adult cattle units (ACU) is strikingly on an increase from 1961 to 1966, 1972, 1977 and 1981 in all districts of Western Rajasthan. The increase in livestock has resulted in decline in the effective area of grazing land available for each livestock. Inspite of low productivity, the arid region sustains a very high population of livestock.The high carrying capacity results in the over use of these lands and in depletion of natural vegetation which necessitates the pastoralists to migrate with their livestock in search of pastures.

Many of the environmental problems today in the arid areas are due to the exponential growth of man's activities. This is no less true in respect of irrational landuse by mankind. The land-use pattern in arid region has traditionally been guided by the conservation-oriented motives. Recent trends, however, reveal that with the increasing intensity of land use the fragile balance between productivity and resource depletion process is gradually disappearing. The data on land utilization for the past 33 years reveal that consistent decadal increase was registered for forests, non-agricultural uses, permanent pastures and net sown area, whereas the same for culturable wastes, current and old fallows, and barren lands registered a considerable decline. Especially from increments in net sown areas, it can be concluded that areas which were hitherto incapable of raising crops and were serving as a valuable resource for livestock raising, were continuously going under the weight of plough.

The economy of the arid region, in general, and its north-western parts, in particular, is dominated by livestock farming. Practically every village had some common pasture lands. **But the State has no legislation reflecting its concern for these grazing lands and there is no coherent pasture policy.** The State Government, through certain post- Independence land reforms coupled with agricultural production drives have resulted into a continuous forced- conversion of wastelands into cropped lands. During last 30 years, barren lands from the 6 districts (Bikaner, Barmer, Jhunjhunu, Nagaur, Pali and Sikar), culturable wastes from all arid districts excepting Barmer and Jaisalmer districts, and long fallows in all eleven arid districts excepting Sri Ganganagar have declined resulting into increased cropping area. Another noteworthy damage that this has caused is on the traditional economic advantage of livestock farming in the region. Arid region of Western Rajasthan is eminently suitable for production of milk, meat, bullocks, wool and other livestock products which are predominantly based on the extensive grazing systems in the arid wastelands. Once the flow of reduction in area is accentuated due to pressure of human population in favour of cultivation, the added geometrical annual growth of about 2.5 percent per annum would have to thrive increasingly on limited area with declining livestock productivity.

The relationship between these developments and the persistence and increase in the pastoral nomadism in the arid regions is a direct one. The elimination of common grazing resource through their privatization reduced the capacity of the pastoralists to sustain their flocks on local resources, making movement outward in search of grazing, even more imperative. So also, the removal of restrictions in the form of levies etc. on the use of common grazing, water and fuel resources, has resulted in the unrestricted and unregulated exploitation of these resources, thereby leading to their rapid deterioration and destruction, with similar effects on pastoral nomadism.

The slow destruction of the country's grazing lands has created serious problems for the management of India's vast animal population. Particularly affected are the nomadic populations. Experts meeting at the UN Conference on Desertification in Nairobi in 1977 agreed unanimously that nomadism and transhumant animal husbandry is the best possible productive system from an ecological point of view for the use of fragile ecoystems in arid and semi-arid areas.

The Government of India, however, does not appear to have accepted this wisdom. It has no real policy for helping nomadic groups adjust to the changing environment or to help them improve it. The general attitude of most government agencies is to devise ways to settle these groups. "The nomads in the present day society prove a menace for the whole society and their sedenterisation is inescapable, States the Department of Environment's State of India's Environment report. Government policies, ecological destruction and growing hostility from the settled populations have forced many nomadic groups to give up nomadism and become landless labourers.

Meanwhile, the natural balance that once existed between environmental resources and stocking rates is now being disturbed. Environmental resources available to nomads have thus diminished noticeably because of inadequate government policies to protect grazing lands and active government policies to push crop production on marginal lands. To ensure their own survival livestock breeders have responded by increasing their animal populations and keeping more browsers. The result is heavier destruction of grazing lands and pressure on forests. The government, therefore, faces its biggest challenge in determining the future development strategy for its nomadic groups and in restoring the country's grazing lands to health.

The answer to the huge problem of the pastoral nomads lies in an appropriate and integrated national land- use plan. So far most attention has been paid to the area under crop cultivation, and very little emphasis on fodder production. The hard fact is that the management of forest lands, grazing lands, croplands and livestock in arid zone cannot be isolated from each other.

Annexures

ANNEXURE-I

DETAILS OF SHEEP MIGRATED FROM EACH DISTRICT FROM 1983 - 84 TO 1989 - 90

(in Lakhs)

Sl. No.	Name of the District	Sheep Population as per 1988	Number of migrated sheep						
			83-84	84-85	85-86	86-87	87-88	88-89	89-90
1.	Jaisalmer	4.84	1.34	0.69	1.44	3.75	8.48	-	0.81
2.	Pali	10.31	1.84	3.49	3.87	4.41	8.00	0.63	0.85
3.	Barmer	4.82	0.46	1.22	0.22	4.08	9.25	-	0.83
4.	Jalore	4.20	0.48	2.55	0.29	3.20	3.55	0.21	0.87
5.	Nagaur	9.27	2.53	2.95	1.65	4.25	9.76	0.83	1.33
6.	Jodhpur	7.69	2.34	2.96	2.45	4.25	9.18	0.78	4.02
7.	Ajmer	5.67	0.65	0.45	0.65	2.12	2.06	-	-
8.	Bikaner	8.23	-	-	1.95	1.82	9.97	-	5.96
9.	Suratgarh	5.37	-	-	0.69	1.50	0.41	-	-
10.	Churu	5.05	-	-	-	1.50	0.76	-	3.09
11.	Sikar	2.93	0.03	-	0.26	1.20	-	-	0.04
12.	Jhunjhunu	2.12	-	-	0.65	0.70	-	-	-
13.	Jaipur	4.06	-	-	0.34	0.93	0.56	-	-
14.	Tonk	3.49	-	-	0.04	1.20	-	0.64	-
15.	Banswara	0.22	-	-	0.13	-	-	-	-
16.	Bhilwara	7.37	-	-	3.10	0.05	-	-	-
17.	Udaipur	3.95	-	-	-	2.65	-	-	-
Temp.Migrated Sheep			10.36		26.93	37.62	61.99	3.09	20.79
Permanent Migrated Sheep			8.50		8.50	10.00	10.00	12.00	12.00
	Total	89.59	18.86		35.43	47.62	71.99	15.09	32.79

Source: Sheep & Wool Dept. Government of Rajasthan, Jaipur.

ANNEXURE-II

DETAILS OF DISTRICTWISE PERMANENT CHECKPOST OF SHEEP MIGRATION

S.No	District		Cheque Post
1.	Kota	1.	Sahabad
		2.	Bhanwargarh
		3.	Bara
		4.	Kailwara
		5.	Darra
		6.	Bora-Bas
2.	Bundi	1.	Indergarh
		2.	Hindoli
		3.	Khadipur
		4.	Dabbi
		5.	Gardada
3.	Jhalawara	1.	Jhalarapatan
		2.	Akkalera
		3.	Khanpur
		4.	Bakkani
		5.	Dag
4.	Chittorgarh	1.	Rawtbhata
		2.	Javda
		3.	Bhansroragarh
		4.	Arnor
		5.	Manderasara
		6.	Pratapgarh
		7.	Bagu
		8.	Chootisadari
		9.	Nibhada
5.	Bhilwara	1.	Tilswamahadava
		2.	Baniya Ka Talab
		3.	Arroli
		4.	Gudda
		5.	Mainal
		6.	Bhopatpura
6.	Sawaimadhopur	1.	Mahuva
7.	Bharatpur	1.	Nagar
		2.	Nadbai

Annexure - III

Honourable Prime Minister of India
New Delhi

Subject: Problems of Pastoral Nomads; building for their future, (Providing relief in grazing charges and regulating grazing of migratoary sheep in the forest of Madhya Pradesh).

Respected Sir,

This memorandum is on behalf of the weakest of the weaker section of the society namely Nomadic Schedule Tribe of Rebarais of Raikas or Dewasies and also Gujars, Jats, Muslims, etc. from Rajasthan and Gujarat.

The migration of men and livestock between complementary ecological zones is a frequent feature of arid and semi-arid regions. The compulsions leading to the emergence and persistence of nomadism in Western Rajasthan and Gujarat derives from its arid environment. It is also well known that the causes behind the increasing incidence of migration from western Rajasthan and Gujarat are intertwined with some of the major historical processes characterizing the region's development.

1. Pastoral nomadic migrations are an age old phenomenon, and until the turn of the last century, the movement of these people into forests, commons and cultivated areas was largely unrestricted by the State and governed more by the system of seasons. The last fifty years have seen an increasing encroachment upon the right of these people to practice their way of life under the guise of various State measures and by broader developmental process.

In 1917 the colonial British Government enacted the Indian Forest Act, which was followed by an extensive exploitation and destruction of our forest wealth by colonial and commercial interests.

2. Migration is increasingly being resorted to by groups not traditionally practicing it, and more significantly it forms the basis of livelihood to a large section of the landless and marginal land holding population of the desert region.

3. At the U.N. Conference on Desertification held in Nairobi in 1977, experts of the problem had unanimously agreed that nomadism and transhumance animal husbandry is the best possible productive system from an ecological point of view for the use of fragile ecosystems in the arid and semi-arid areas. In contarst, we have the Govt. of India's official attitude exemplified in their quotation from the "**State of India's Environment**": "The nomads of the present day society prove a menace for the whole of society and their sedentarization is inescapable". This sharp difference in stands is indicative of a failure to appreciate the fine ecological balance which can be achieved by pastoral nomadic adaptation and its considerable potential for maximization of the nation's income and well-being.

4. Today the pastoral nomad is being required to pay for the destructive capacity, of colonial and commercial interests and what is worse, he is being held responsible for the destruction, while the political context of a colonial State no longer exists, the attitude of the State vis-a-vis the interests of these pastoral nomadic groups remains unchanged. Very little though has been given at higher levels in planning for the future of these peoples. A major drought, temporarily weakens the powers that be, from their apathy, which does not however, result in any long-term planning. If anything, systematic discrimination has been the official policy. It is not the building of dams, and mines, for extending an under-productive agriculture that is being seen as the enemy of our forests. Instead, the migratory shepherd has been made the convenient scape-goat.

Today, the total number of sheep in Rajasthan is around one crore. Their produce of wool in valued at between 20 to 25 crores of Rupees. About 40 lakh mutton sheep worth 30 crore of Rupees are slaughtered each year. 7 to 8 lakh people are solely dependent on their way of life of nomadism. We may stress then that the considerable scale of their migratory way of life, as well as the poverty of the social groups that practice it warrants that their problems cannot be dismissed as out dated or irrelevant. There is need today for a fresh approach to the problem. An enlightened view instead, would consider both the reasons for the existing State policy as well as alternative and appropriate points and directions in governmental intervention.

It is against this background that we list few problems faced by the shepherds:

(a) These shepherds face an increasing competition from the relatively uneconomic cultivation of the marginal agricultural lands, in effect, indirectly contributing to the making of poorer economic returns of the nation's resources than possible.

(b) In the quest of developing the nation's forest resources there has been a brutal lack of sensitivity about the welfare of these people. The shepherds and the flocks are not necessarily a threat to conservation, their system of grazing is highly sensitive to the needs of regenerating pasture and forest produce, and what is more they contribute significantly through fertilising the areas in which they graze.

(c) There has been an equally insensitive attitude on the question of handling the inter-state movements that are a necessary part of this adaptation. In particular, the neighbouring State of Madhya Pradesh has shown an impertinent callousness in its discriminatory treatment of the shepherds and the flocks. This fact has been acknowledged by the Supreme Court.

(d) These shepherds and their families also face discrimination through a lack of political representation. There exist at present no major political forums, which my articulate their needs and interests. This is further compounded by their almost total lack of literacy, education and the relative isolation of their lives.

(e) While these shepherds contribute in important ways to the nation's economy, their own condition physical, material and financial- is in the main, relatively weak. For the great majority of shepherds, it is a subsistence economy; indebtedness is high and their exploitation by market mechanisms, middlemen and even the petty bureaucract is often tyrranical.

(f) In the course of seeking their livelihood, these men, women and children have to face dangers from many quarters. Thefts of the animals are not an infrequent feature. This often results in conflicts,where shepherds become the victims of local biases.

While the current situation gives much cause to worry there is also much that is encouraging. The nomadic shepherd is fast becoming conscious of his rights. It is important that their awareness be further nurtured and encouraged. This can only be done by initiative on the part of the State and the people's representatives of the States of Gujarat and Rajasthan, and its neighbourhood. It is suggested that a Commission be set up to enquire into the problems of these people, composed of concerned individuals of repute and integrity form these states.

Ever since the introduction of Madhya Pradesh Grazing Rates Rules 1979 the problems of Nomads have aggrevated. Litigation success of the Nomads in the Supreme Court in 1982 made the State Govt. vindictive, and it took stringent measures to multiply and aggravate the sufferings of Nomads rather than alleviating them.

Having exhausted all other avenues, we are now approaching the Prime Minister of India, who is the highest executive authority in the country.

We request for short-term, long term and immediate measures, relief as follows:

I **Immediate Measures:**

Without considering the net income derived from per sheep or per goat per year, (in absence of any scientific economic study) the Madhya Pradesh Govt. has abnormally raised the grazing charges to the tune of one thousand per cent during the year 1986. Since 1979 the grazing charge per sheep per year was Rupee one which has been increased to Rupees ten, similarly the grazing charges of goat has been increased from Rupees one to ten Rupees and for camel from Rupees ten to Rupees fifty per head per year.

In other states the grazing charge per sheep or goat is only 0.50 paisa to Rs.1.00 per annum.

The high rates fixed by Madhya Pradesh Govt. cannot be paid by the migratory sheep farmers as the income derived from sheep or goat per year is not more than one or two rupees. This point is to be considered at all level so that the grazing charges for sheep and goat could be charged at the rate of rupee one per head per year and for camel at the rate of rupees ten.

On account of increasing the grazing charges by State of Madhya Pradesh the poor sheep farmers had to take the shelter of the Supreme Court and the High Court at Jabalpur. Unless the authority of the Prime Minister is used to consider this burning problem, the Chief Minister of Madhya Pradesh is not going to revise the grazing rates.

II. **Short-term Measures:**

1. A high power co-ordination Committee consisting of officers from the Government of India and States of Rajasthan, Madhya Pradesh, Gujarat, Uttar Pradesh, Haryana, Andhra Pradesh, Maharashtra, Orissa etc. and the prominent leaders of migratory sheep farmers and other sheep farmers, be constituted to co- ordinate and regulate migration of sheep.
2. Grazing fee for sheep, goats and camels should be made uniform in different States and be within the paying capacity of the poor sheep farmers.
3. Definite forest areas for grazing should be defined in different States.

   Like wild life sanctuaries in forest areas now we should introduce sheep sanctuaries in forest areas of all States.
4. Police protection should be provided on migratory routes and grazing areas to prevent theft of sheep.
5. A large number of sheep die due to epidemics and diseases. Mobile veterinary services should be provided on routes of sheep migration and grazing areas.
6. The sheep farmers get the value of wool, and mutton sheep to the tune of 25 to 40 per cent only and the remaining profit of 60 to 75 per cent is earned by middleman. Therefore, some marketing organisation for wool and mutton sheep should be formed.

III. **Long-term Measures:**

1. Ranches and large areas should be developed within Rajasthan and Gujarat so that the number of sheep going on migration is reduced drastically. At present almost all sheep farmers are landless or having small pieces of lands, which are uneconomical.
2. Migration rotues within Rajasthan should be worked out and facilities of water, shelter, shearing spots, storage, of wool etc. should be created.
3. A massive programme for upgrading the sheep should be taken up so that the present population of sheep may be

reduced without affecting the income of individual sheep farmer and the national income.

4. Almost all the stationary and migratory sheep farmers are illiterate who have not been covered by the agency of Adult Education. Thus a separate special sheme has to be framed so that unemployed literate persons could be employed to remain with the groups of migratory sheep farmers to educate the adults as well as children who lead camp life in common open areas of jungles.

We, therefore, request that the Prime Minister may kindly direct the Chief Minister of Madhya Pradesh to revise the grazing charges at earliest otherwise we will not be in position to pay the grazing charges of sheep at rate of rupees ten per year per sheep and rupees fifty for camel, without ruining our tribes.

Thanking you, Sir,

Sd/-

(GHUMAKAR BHED PALAK SANGH)

PRESIDENT

ANNEXURE-IV

NATIONAL WORKSHOP ON SHEEP MIGRATION
6 - 7 FEBRUARY, 1991

RECOMMENDATIONS

1. For regulating sheep migration in an organised way there should be coordination at the administrative heads level, of different departments of the States related to sheep migration for providing proper security and other facilities to the sheep farmers like health cover, watering and marketing of wool, meat and animals etc.
2. Services centres may be established on migration routes for providing services enumerated under "1" above.
3. Separate department should be created in every sheep rich State for establishing contacts and paying proper attention for the development of sheep and sheep farmers so that they are encouraged to adopt improved sheep breeding, management and health care delivery systems.
4. Each of the important sheep rearing states should develop appropriate long term strategy for sheep improvement with well defined time bound targets and develop suitable extension system to achieve the same.
5. The matters and disputes relating to sheep migration may be brought under the purview of Inter-state Council and grazing tariff charged should be nominal.
6. Wool should be declared as Agricultural produce and included in the NCDC Charter. The Agric. Price Commission may fix the national support price for wool.
7. Pasture Development and Fodder Production Corporations should be established at the State and National level.
8. Migration of sheep to the adjacent States may be minised by establishing silvi-pastures for sheep within the States. In each State, reserve grazing during lean seasons. In Rajasthan the West Bank of IGNP may be allotted for this purpose.

9. Established pastures may be managed by the Panchayats. Sheep Farmers Cooperatives, Forest departments/Pasture Development Corporation.
10. Sheep farmers may be given subsidy and bank loans for establishing pastures and growing fodder trees on their own lands.
11. Sheep should be included in the list of the animals entitled for fodder subsidy and other concessions during famine as applicable for cattle.
12. At present as per Rajasthan Tenancy Act sheep and goats are not counted in a village population for keeping Gochar land. In village only large animals'numbers are counted. The Rajasthan Tenancy Act should be amended accordingly and sufficient area for grazing sheep should be kept in every village to check heavy migration.
13. At present, sheep are not allowed for grazing in the reserved pastures developed by Forest Department Panchayats. Sheep should also be allowed for grazing in these areas.